The Chambered Nautilus
Oliver Wendell Holmes
1858

This is the ship of pearl, which, poets feign,
Sails the unshadowed main,—
The venturous bark that flings
On the sweet summer wind its purpled wings
In gulfs enchanted, where the Siren sings,
And coral reefs lie bare,
Where the cold sea-maids rise to sun their streaming hair.

Its webs of living gauze no more unfurl;
Wrecked is the ship of pearl!
And every chambered cell,
Where its dim dreaming life was wont to dwell,
As the frail tenant shaped his growing shell,
Before thee lies revealed,—
Its irised ceiling rent, its sunless crypt unsealed!

Year after year beheld the silent toil
That spread his lustrous coil;
Still, as the spiral grew,
He left the past year's dwelling for the new,
Stole with soft step its shining archway through,
Built up its idle door,
Stretched in his last-found home, and knew the old no more.

Thanks for the heavenly message brought by thee,
Child of the wandering sea,
Cast from her lap, forlorn!
From thy dead lips a clearer note is born
Than ever Triton blew from wreathèd horn!
While on mine ear it rings,
Through the deep caves of thought I hear a voice that sings:—

Build thee more stately mansions, O my soul,
As the swift seasons roll!
Leave thy low-vaulted past!
Let each new temple, nobler than the last,
Shut thee from heaven with a dome more vast,
Till thou at length art free,
Leaving thine outgrown shell by life's unresting sea!

The Book of Nothing

*Breakthrough Nondual Quotes
& Questions*

FRED DAVIS

The Book of Nothing
From Awakening to Abidance
© 2021 Fred Davis

Published in the US by Awakening Clarity Press

ISBN 13: 979-8-52197713-0

Cover design and interior design by www.jimandzetta.com

Compiled by Gordon Goodman

Edited by Kathleen Sutherland, John Wiersba & Mike Lilly

Adapted and expanded by the author

Thanks to Jane Cockerell & Betsy Hackett-Davis for their vital contributions

Dedicated to the memory of Gordon "Tim" Goodman, M.D., who selflessly devoted himself to the transcription of these quotes from the original satsang recordings

Foreword

Although Fred Davis has authored five successful books, many would agree that his greatest gifts as a teacher are most prominent in his personal interactions with students: leading them in inquiry and pointing toward our shared true nature. This book, a collection of Fred's questions and pointers from his weekly online satsang gatherings, presents that direct approach in written form.

Fred Davis considers himself an *unteacher*. His task is simply to lift the veil to reveal...*nothing*. This book is just that, *The Book of Nothing*. Phrase by phrase, all that we think we know is swept away. We are left with nothing to stand on, nothing to lean on. Nothing to get in the way. Nothing at all. And so we behold our exquisite True Nature—empty, clear, and free.

Central to this approach, which is a departure from most teachings, is that we can awaken only now. We *are* awake now. We are *Awakeness* now. Don't make your awakening a story of future. See the truth of what you are, no matter how fleeting the glimpse. Then let that realization deepen and broaden as you work to gain clarity. Essentially, this involves thinning the ego, the illusory sense of separate self, which Fred refers to as the "character" or "unit."

This book leads us into our True Nature, with pointers and questions to help us see that we are already awake, that we are Awakeness itself. It then reveals how to hold steady in our realization of truth, while integrating our vision of the absolute into everyday life—the world and its ongoing stories. Throughout, we are gently reminded that none of this—awakening, abidance, integration—can be found anywhere or at any time other than here and now. This is a great blessing. As Fred often reminds us, "It doesn't get any better than this!"

In reading this book, proceed slowly. Savor the unveiling. You are not gathering information. Awakening is about unlearning, unknowing. As with Zen koans, the truth echoes in the space and silence between the words, between your thoughts. It's about letting yourself go and allowing yourSelf to shine. It's about nothing, absolutely nothing.

Kathleen Sutherland, Editor

Introduction

The quotes in this book come primarily from Sunday Satsang. Many of these quotes have served to bring spiritual seekers worldwide to initial awakening. Other passages here have helped facilitate "clearing," or the path we walk following our awakening. The power of satsang after we awaken cannot be overstated.

Contrary to popular belief, many people *do* awaken to True Nature. However, precious few clear up afterward. This book can help you with both pre- and post-awakening. Any bit of micro-fame this Teaching enjoys has primarily arisen due to word of mouth about me being the "wake-you-up-right-now" guy. However, 80% of my time is spent working with people after awakening has already taken place.

I recommend that you approach this volume seriously and read it slowly and thoughtfully. Consider making it a practice; put it by your bedside or near your favorite reading chair. Become one of those "precious few."

I hear a lot of people say that "all nondual teachers are saying the same thing." That's not true. The *pointing* may all be in the same *direction*, but it's certainly *not* all the same. I can help you get to my backyard by *telling you* to start in my living room and then circumnavigate the globe. Or I can take you by the arm, walk you out my back door, and *show* it to you.

There are countless gradations of clarity and skillfulness within the teaching community. Nisargadatta Maharaj often said about his Teaching, *"You will not find this elsewhere."* I say the same.

I teach the theory and methodology of The Living Method to students in my teacher training program, but I could not in a million years tell you *why* it works. And frankly, I don't *care* why it works. It *does*. I have witnessed well over a thousand awakenings, and every single one of them has been the apparent result of nondual inquiry.

There are tons of pointers in nonduality, but I notice most of them point in the wrong direction. The rediscovery of our True Nature is *so simple*. However, we consistently privilege *thoughts about* our experience over the *facts* of our experience. Thus, we fail to see the forest for the trees. This Teaching reverses that.

Shortly after the awakening that occurred here in 2006, it was seen clearly that seekers didn't need any more *information*. They already had too much! What was needed was a new *presentation*. Repetition is the mother of clarity, and you will find some here. It's a tap-tap-tapping that leads to what feels like a "sudden breakthrough."

As you read, it's good to remember that most of the quotes were initially part of a larger, longer conversation with kindred spirits. To assist the reader, I have provided some sense of context wherever I felt it was needed. However, remember that verbal teachings are always the slaves of language; don't become a slave to it yourself. Use a raft to cross the river, and then abandon it on the far side.

And now I will let the quotes speak for themselves. May they hit you like a hammer.

Fred Davis
March 1, 2021

- No Beginning -

1. If you look closely, you'll see that many teachings consist of having the "enlightened wonder" sitting on a dais or some other kind of throne-like device instructing a group of tragically "unenlightened students" on how to wake up to True Nature.

That *can't* happen; it is *impossible*. There is *no such thing as* an "enlightened unit" or an "unenlightened unit."

The fiction of enlightened or unenlightened *units* may be due to a misunderstanding by the students, which causes a false projection. This happens a lot. Or it may be an *intentional* image encouraged by a less than clear teacher. Regardless, I've noticed that this is a very common delusion in nonduality today. It is the invisible mote in nearly everyone's eye.

I say that because, whether given or taken, this confused "front-door" (awaken the unit-character) approach appears to be the default teaching "model," both historically and today. Speaking in general terms, that model *doesn't work*. It *can't*. The fox is left guarding the henhouse.

Some followers will wake up on their own *despite* such teaching, but it's unlikely anyone will wake up *from* it. I'm quite aware this sounds like modern heresy.

So be it.

2. *What* are you?

What are you—*really*?

The knowledge of what you are is all you need to Know.

It is also all there *is* to Know.

This Knowledge is available only Here and Now.

No one has ever woken up "soon."

3. It's so simple you could miss it—and we almost invariably do. It is always here and always clear. It is *This*, and *This* is *You*.

4. *This* is What Is. "What isn't" is simply the content of your imagination. Without comparing What Is to "what isn't," how are things going right now?

5. Believing in the reality of our imagination is the only bondage. The willingness to see and acknowledge this truth is all that's necessary for your freedom.

6. A "personal me" attempting to *think about* what I am is a fatally flawed activity from the outset. There is no real "personal me" here that could either think or fail to think. In fact, the entire story of a "personal me" is just an unowned, conditioned thought stream. That thought stream is *itself* conditioning.

7. To notice the freedom that is already available, we have to remain open to *unknowing* most of what we think we know.

8. We believe we are the unit-character with its apparent thoughts, beliefs, opinions, and positions. We believe we are this sack of conditioning called a human being. That belief is tantamount to falling down the rabbit hole.

9. Everything in authentic spirituality works exactly 180 degrees away from how we think it does. So I often refer to this Teaching as "The Backward Teaching."

10. This false sense of division is what we must come to see through *in the now*—over and over again. Enlightenment has neither past nor future.

We do this by relentlessly turning our gaze back on itself. Awakening is when attention—*focused* awareness—recognizes the boundless field of *unfocused* awareness as *itself*.

11. Right now, this moment, could you prove to me that you are *not* awake?

12. Close your eyes. Notice that you're looking at a dark field. Once you recognize that the dark field has neither boundaries nor limits of any kind, could you ever locate a *center* to it?

Can you be *outside* of it?

13. Within the scope of the dream of relativity-ness, we believe we see a "this" here, a "that" over there. We see them as *objects* because we unconsciously project them; we *project* a dualistic "reality" that does not exist, and which never did and never will. Until there is Self-Realization and some degree of clearing, we habitually self-validate the false sense of a "me" as being true in just this same way.

14. The *neti-neti* process we've all heard about (but only a small number have ever seriously utilized) means inquiring into what we are *not*. We test everything present to discover *experientially* that whatever it is that we *are*, we certainly are *not* this particular arising, or that one, or the other one, or any relative object at all.

Indeed, "We" is *unfindable*. We first need to see *What Isn't* before we can see What Is. Typically, we grow tired of such questioning in a few minutes or a few days. I didn't.

Meet thought with a rigorous, persistent, and skillful nondual inquiry, and you stand a wonderful chance of meeting Life As It Is. Once you see what isn't true, Truth shines on its own. *You can't miss it.*

15. Tell me, can you imagine what was happening just *before* the Big Bang? The mind can't go there, can it?

16. However, there can't be a "me" unless there is also an "other." Mentally, we take Oneness and "break it" into two pieces, naming the first mental projection "me" and the second mental projection "other."

Wherever I say "we," that "we" is something akin to the *royal* "we." It's referring to Not-Two.

17. Is the *sense* of something the same thing as the *truth* of something?

A *sense* of something doesn't *necessarily* point to the *truth* of anything, does it?

18. So, in the absence of a "self-center," what *do* we find?

Is it not this immediate, non-locatable *sense* of being, the *feeling* of your very own presence?

Is it more or less just an aware-*ing*—a seeing/being—without attributes itself and beyond definition?

Can anything exist, be known, or be experienced in the *absence* of this sense of being?

19. Truth is quite apparent, quite simple. The only real "work" to be done is to remain free of our former concepts, thus allowing the unfettered truth to shine by itself.

This activity is what I term "clearing." It's the *un*believing of unconscious, false patterns.

20. Common misunderstandings exhibit an endless array of fallacies:

"Time" and "space" appear to exist and even be meaningful.
"Hierarchy" is thought of as being a useful tool in the service of "organization."

"Important" is believed to be a useful descriptor.
"Here" and "there" seem to relate to something.

"Good and bad" are meaningful.
"Past and future" exist.

As clarity arises within post-awakening, we can't help but notice that none of these are even remotely true.

21. Given that we can find no boundary to This (whatever it is), then clearly it has no center. Did you (whatever it is that you are) think *yourself* to be the center?

22. Even in the heart of a dedicated and skillful inquiry, we may find that the investigation is based on an erroneous assumption, which can only lead to erroneous results.

23. Nonduality is about first *recognizing* and then *accepting* True Nature, *As It Is*. No one does it; it just appears to happen within the dream of relativity-ness.

24. *Neti-neti,* "not this, not this" is a very old and powerful means of discovering what we are *not*. We need to see *what isn't* before we can see *What Is*. Meet thought with rigorous nondual inquiry, and you meet Life As It Is.

25. The easiest way to find out what you *are* is to be crystal clear about what you *are not*.

You are *not* the body, the mind, the personality, or the world. What you are is neither awake nor failing to be awake.

There is no such thing as either an awakened character or unit. There is only Awakeness—conscious of Itself or not—which has no capacity for sleep.

26. Realization is just finally noticing what has been here all along.

27. There is much *less* here than meets the eye.

28. You are the Unborn, Unbound, Untouched.

29. What can you know prior to the sense of being?

30. You are not the body, the mind, or the personality.

What you are is neither awake nor failing to be awake.

There is no such thing as an awakened character or unit. There is only *Awakeness*, which has no capacity for sleep.

Awakeness can show up as any form, including the interior form of a character or the exterior form of a unit.

31. Every moment we spend looking *for* True Nature, we are already looking *from, past,* and *through* True Nature without recognizing it.

32. Imagine a hurricane. Let's call it Hurricane Bob. Hurricane Bob is composed of broad bands of heavy weather and its accompanying drama: floods, tornadoes, lightning, and thunder. It feels like the very *essence* of Hurricane Bob should be right in the dead center of the weather bands.

Yet when the National Oceanic and Atmospheric Administration flies planes into the heart of a hurricane, they find no-thing. There is no-thing in the center of that activity. Where it *seems* like a center should be, there is only an absence of a storm.

33. Right now, could you prove to me that you are *not* awake? How would you go about doing that?

34. Oneness, do you think you *are* that body? Or perhaps you feel you're somehow *contained in* that body?

Do you think that human body—that *animated cadaver*—is something *outside* Oneness? If it were, wouldn't that have to be at least *two-ness*?

There's just the one and only You. Will you notice that you *can only be* Oneness itself?

My dear Oneness, have you been waiting for some *other, different* Oneness? You know, the *cooler-than-This-Right-Now* Oneness, the *mystical* Oneness.

Did you, at some point in time, experience *a cooler-than-This-Right-Now* Oneness, that you then lost?

Tell me, my dear Oneness, can Oneness *lose* itself?

Can Oneness *fall out of* itself?

Can Oneness oscillate between itself and something that is not itself?

Where could you, Oneness, *go* when you believe that you're oscillating?

35. There are no rules here because there is only this *Hereness As It Is*; there is no "other" to make, break, or follow any rules. *This As It Is* has no alternative and no comparison.

36. I am the Unborn, the One Without a Second, prior to and beyond history or future, birth or death, heaven or hell. There is no opposite to Me. I, Awakeness, know nothing about this rumor of death. It is *not* experienceable.

Experience tells us that units come and units go and within the ways of the world, this is true.

However, units—regardless of how charming or attractive they might be—are vacant, animated corpses. They are tools for vicarious experiencing. They seem to appear, they seem to disappear, yet they neither live nor die.

37. When did this presently-felt sense of being first arise?
Investigate that.

38. What can you absolutely, positively recall *prior* to the birth of that body?

39. If you can feel or remember past lives, *whose* past lives were they?

40. Fred Davis has not incarnated thus far, and I have no reason to believe such a thing could happen later.

41. Emptiness is unscathed by *what isn't.*

42. Is it possible that the "I Am" principle is a *doorway* and not a *destination?*

43. When a rainbow ceases to shine, is there any need to mourn or bury it?

44. Most spiritual seekers *want* to be seekers who genuinely want to wake up. Yet, most of them are not.

45. First, we come to see what we are *not*. We are not these bodies through which the Tao operates.

We are not these arising thoughts—which are *processed* by but are not *initiated* by the brain.

We are not the emotions that play through the bodies that we *think* we are. We are not any kind of physical being in search of consciousness.

We are consciousness, thinking it is a single human being, in *search* of consciousness. How long do you think consciousness can *search* for consciousness like this?

46. Imaginary beings make up imaginary rules in an imaginary world. Within this dream, Awakeness comes to believe that it is one—*just one*—of the imaginary beings. We call this misidentification, and it is the source of all seeking and suffering.

Once the misidentification bait has been swallowed, belief then "confirms" it as being valid. One thought confirms another, as is *always* the case. A sense of separation falls into place and suffering arises.

It is entirely circular and completely nuts.

This is why I say that I can only wake up "crazy people." If you don't know who you are, then you are, by definition, insane. It doesn't matter how nice or good you are or how much you help out the imaginary beings in the make-believe world.

If Mother Teresa had been unaware of her True Nature, she'd have been just a crazy do-gooder from India. What's the harm in that? There is no harm in it at all unless the older Mother Teresa unit happened to be *a seeking unit*, as it was in its youth. If *that's* the case, there will be untold suffering until this misidentification is rooted out and left in full sunlight. Just like the vampire it is, ego disappears when exposed to light.

That's our job here: to bring confusion and suffering out into the open and expose them. That's *all* we have to do. A malignant tumor will die on its own when there is nothing left for it to devour.

47. Regardless of the form of the present arising, it cannot be *other* than you, but it is never *equal* to you.

48. You don't need this arising or its content, but this arising can't even *exist* without You. In the absence of the sense of being what can exist?

49. *What is it* that's reading this sentence?

50. Speaking off the cuff, does that body contain you, or do You contain that body?

51. Can you *locate* the self you've always thought yourself to be?

Or does your so-called "location" always seem to be somewhere you're *not* looking?

52. I know there's a tingling behind your eyes, and it seems that it might be you, but are you truly *inside* of that head? Is it possible for your skull to be a "fence" that holds Oneness entrapped inside? Does that make *any* sense at all?

53. In your search for True Nature, do you know what you're looking *for*?
If not, how will you ever know that you've found it?
Most importantly, do you know *what's looking*?

54. Look carefully at any so-called object.

Can you actually *find* a separation between *what's looking* and what's being *looked at*?

No, you can't. I've seen hundreds of people try, and nobody can. However, anybody can *make up* lines of demarcation, but that doesn't make them true.

Can you even find *two separate things*, or do you find only a *single continuum*? I already know. *You* check.

I think you'll find that there's no "looker" and no "looked at"; there is only *looking*. Notice that you're a verb, not a noun.

What would be another name for this single continuum?

Yes, another name for it is Oneness.

(You can't successfully *think* your way to an accurate conclusion. *Do the exercise.*)

55. Can you offer any *evidence* to prove your most cherished beliefs are true, or is there just a conditioned habit of automatically *deferring* to them?

56. *Right this moment,* if you momentarily drop the lie that you are that unit, can you—whatever that is— experience either space or time?

57. Is the statement "I Am" merely an example of false referencing?

58. Is space what *separates* everything from everything else, or is it actually the *glue* that holds "everything" *together?*

59. Can you find anything *outside* of awareness?
Could you *ever* find anything outside of awareness?
Is that even *possible?*

Is space *outside* or *inside* of awareness?
You are boundless—really boundlessness itself—meaning there *is no* "outside" to you.

Without an "outside" does the term "inside" make any sense?

Is Awareness distinct from what it is aware *of?*

60. You do not come and go. You do not live or die. However, you don't Know *yourSelf* in the absence of consciousness. Without consciousness, there can be no "sense of being," which is what consciousness is. Without the sense of being, there can be neither knower, nor known, nor even knowing.

Are you sentient, or are you *sentience itself*, patterning Off and On?

61. Is it possible for Oneness to either expand or contract?

62. When you are feeling expansive, tell me, *whose* sense of expansion is it? Can you find an *owner* of that sense of expansion?

63. How much does an *appearance* weigh?
How much do *you* weigh?
I'm not asking about the body's weight; I'm asking about *Yours.*

64. You need this world to know yourself objectively, but do you genuinely *need* to know yourself objectively?

Don't *think—check! Right now.*

65. Why don't you go ahead and *notice* True Nature?
What is it that tries to notice True Nature?

Can you see that I'm asking *True Nature* to notice True Nature?
There's nothing *other* than True Nature to ask, and no one to ask or to be asked.

There is nothing *other* than True Nature. You are *It.*

66. In your own experience *right now*, does True Nature feel more like a *noun*, or is it more like a *verb*?

67. Basic humility for me is to confess that I don't know what I am. I don't even know *what it is* that doesn't know what it is!

68. Ask yourself, "Do I need the world?"
Then tell yourself the truth.

69. Do you need that body? Do you truly need anything at all?

In the absence of the belief in a "personal me", can you find any actual lack? Is there anything missing? Broken? Misplaced?

Notice that a *sense* of something does not equal the *truth* of anything. The *sense* of lack you *feel* is not the same as an *actual* lack, any more than the sense of a "personal me" equals the truth of a "personal me".

70. How much *space* does a rainbow take up? What is its *volume*?
Is it *really* there, or is it just conditioning meeting circumstance?

71. There is *no* character. It feels like you are either that body or something *contained* by that body. It's not true. This is how you lie to yourself.

There is no "big" you, no "little" you, no one there to take either credit or blame.

There is just This As It Is—*whatever* This is.

72. Close your eyelids.
Notice the dark field that surrounds you.
What can you notice that is *outside* of that dark field?
Is the body outside of the dark field?
Is the body outside of awareness?

Does awareness have a center?
Remember that a *sense* of a center does not equate with an *actual* center.
Can you find an *edge* to awareness?
Would you agree that a decent definition of a "center" is a point that is equidistant from the edges of a field?

In the absence of an edge, can a center even *exist*?

73. Does it make any sense to inquire about the *height* of a desert mirage whose *appearance* is that of a mountain?

74. A rainbow can't exist without the sky, but the sky doesn't need a rainbow.
You are like the sky. The world is your rainbow.

75. You are *always* Awakeness itself! Can more seeking possibly bring you closer to that which you already are?

76. Fred Davis desperately wanted to discover the truth of God.
But instead, the truth of God discovered the fiction of Fred Davis.

77. *What is it* that is reading this sentence?

78. *This* cannot come to understand *This.*
And there is nothing *other than* This that could ever "understand" This!

79. What Is *is*.
And then we're out of words.

80. The false *sense* of a "personal me" is the core dream of Awakeness.
You are Awakeness dreaming that you are a Susan or a Bob who is looking for Awakeness!

81. Once it is seen that the character is wholly imaginary, *what is it* that sees this?

82. Can you find an *owner* behind your sense of existence?
Don't think your answer through—*check for yourself!*
Right now!

83. Do you notice that in the absence of an imaginary "me" *you're* still here?

84. Is the unit a *reader,* or is the unit the vehicle *through which* apparent reading occurs?

85. What could exist in a vacuum of experience—in the lack of *your very own presently present sense of existence?*

86. Yes, there is undoubtedly a strong *sense* of existence Here/Now, but is a *sense* of something the same thing as a *fact* of anything?

87. You say, "I Am."
I ask, "In the absence of the sense of being, could you know that—or anything else?"

88. There is no center or circumference, no height or weight, and no volume or duration to an illusion. Measurement of an illusion is itself an illusion.

89. Where I come from, we call something that has no measurement or duration an *idea*.

90. Initial awakening is not necessarily confined to, but will at least *include*, the unveiling of the false nature of a separate, distinct "personal me."

91. The notion of a "personal me" is just a belief. It's not even *your* belief. Conditioning automatically arises to meet circumstance, and we declare this movement to be "mine."

Then we give that robotic pattern a *name*, such as "driving," "cooking," or "worrying." In truth, within the born world of relativity-ness, everything is just *happening*, all on its own.

92. Upon recognition of True Nature, it is seen that there simply *is no separate, independent,* so-called "character."

There is no "personal me" that could ever come to "see *This.*"

Awakeness comes to notice *Itself*, and we call that "awakening."

This activity is a cosmic joke.

93. *Right now,* in the *absence* of a "personal me", what do you find?

94. We have always believed—without a single crumb of evidence—that buried somewhere within us was *something* that constituted a "personal me." Yet upon investigation, we see that this "me-idea" was just another thought. That thought was falsely referencing yet another thought.

And so on and so on—back, back, back.

95. If you had to prove to a jury that you are an *independent entity,* how would you go about doing that?

I've done this inquiry a thousand times, if not more. I promise that you *cannot* do so. It's a totally erroneous, absolutely *core* assumption that has confounded you ever since the first day of your "*seekership.*"

96. Stop fretting about *who* you are for a moment.

Regardless of who or what you are, ask yourself instead, "*Where* am I?"

Go *look*. Do it *now*, but only if you're tired of suffering.

Is this so-called "you" *locatable*?

Of course not.
The *seeker* is the *sought*.
(Even if you answer "here", is that a *place*, or is it *You*?)

97. When we look for the "personal me"—when we rest as stillness and investigate—we find only *no*-thing. It's not *something*, but neither is it *nothing*. It's not a noun; it's more like a *verb*.

98. Who or what is experiencing the content of this present arising?

99. Just for a moment, *pretend* to accept Oneness as a fact, even if you can only do so intellectually.

The incredibly obvious, yet almost always overlooked, principle of the Math of One states unequivocally that one equals one (1 = 1).

Given this, *what* is it that has to have been looking for Oneness for all these years?

100. Is Oneness *outside* of Awareness?
Is Awareness *outside* of Oneness?

101. If we had a nondual dictionary, do you think we'd be able to even *find* the word "outside" within it?

102. What is the *one thing* that attention never pays any attention to?

Would you agree that a decent definition of "attention" might be "focused awareness"?

If you accept this definition, are you not acknowledging that awareness has been looking for awareness?

103. When I look around, I don't see *sameness*, but I do see *Oneness*. I see differences in *appearance*, but not in *substance*.

How about *you*?

104. No matter which direction I look in or how long I look, I cannot see anything but "me."

Whatever that is.

105. Given that there is only *One* thing going on here, is there any way you can report to me that you are *not* it?

106. There is a sense of existence—a raw sense of being—is there not?
And it has *always* been with you, has it not?
Take a good look. Can you find an *owner* of that feeling of being?

107. Can you see that That which notices change is itself changeless?

108. Ever since the day you first took a wrong turn into nonduality, you've been told over and over again, "You are not the body."

Have you considered that it might *literally* be true? Pretend for a moment that it is. What happens if you just take the words at face value instead of brainiac-ing for a hidden meaning?

If you even momentarily *pretend* to accept that you are not the body, *what's left?*

109. We need not look for stillness and silence because we are already That which is beyond stillness and silence. Stillness and silence are concepts.

You are not a concept. You are prior to all language and concepts.

110. Now that awakening has happened, are you ready and willing to accept the fact that you are Awake*ness*, *even when you don't feel like it?*

111. Awakeness is not an object; it is the *mother* of all objects.

112. It's not enough to simply *recognize* True Nature. We must then begin to *welcome* the ramifications of that recognition and *abandon* the mindless search for it.

113. Silence is the background upon which *noise* appears and disappears.

114. Stillness is the background upon which "movement" appears and disappears.

115. You are Home ItSelf.

116. Keep returning to this question: *Who is it* that so desperately wants to wake up? Ask, keep asking, and don't let it go until the answer shows itself. But only if you sincerely want to wake up.

117. The Mystery will never unveil itself to the character you believe yourself to be. It's impossible.

Hence the term "*Self*-realization" is properly written only with the use of a capital "S."

118. Behind and beneath the eyes you are looking *with* is the "I" you're looking _for_.

119. The second we identify as the body-mind, we are *already* down the rabbit hole. Once we're at the bottom of the tunnel, we remember that in nonduality, there are tricky things known as "rabbit holes," and we are on the lookout for them!

120. Close your eyes and relax.
Notice that there is a dark field. Only.
It is empty of form, but it's not just empty; it's also full.

Where are *you* in this picture?
Is it possible for you to be *outside* of the dark field when there is *only* the field?

Is it possible for you to be *inside* of the dark field when there is *only* the field?
Do inside and outside have any relevance at all?

Do the concepts of space and time mean anything here in the field? Does this field have either "purpose" or "intent?"

And what of *you?*
Are you *other than* the dark field?

121. How can you ever make real "spiritual progress" when the first step you take on the so-called spiritual path is a step *away* from the truth?

True Nature is looking for True Nature. How's that working out for you so far?

122. In nonduality, doubt is our friend. Sureness is the death of spiritual insight. Awakening is not about what we know. It is about what we *don't* know.

123. *Be still and notice* that this world is not your imaginary character's dream. It's not "your" dream. That is the second most common misunderstanding.

The number one misunderstanding is the belief that there *is* a character to begin with, and that *You* are it. There isn't, and *You* aren't.

124. Manifestation is not the character's dream. The character *is* the dream! Your core dream is that you're a human being living in space and time. You are dreaming that you're an actor in a play!

You—sweet, innocent Awakeness—through the process of divine hypnosis, come to believe that instead of being *all* things and more, you are just *one tiny constituent component*—a particular human being!

Your parents and your community basically "brainwashed" you. It took them about two years of conscious reinforcement to get you to believe it; straight out of the womb, the experience was simply one of unowned awe and wonder.

Think for a moment about video games. They are successful because they allow for a new, imaginary identity to have a virtual, yet realistic and believable, experience in a 3D world.

Do you know where the phenomenon of virtual reality occurs?
It occurs right here, in *this* virtual reality.

125. Realization requires the willingness to have the rug pulled out from underneath you.
Not once, but over and over again.
Every day and *right now!*
And now, and now, and now...

126. You are Existence Itself dreaming that you're exclusively a Fred or a Lucy or a Bob. You move between unknowingly experiencing yourSelf as unconscious Awakeness and knowingly experiencing yourself as Conscious Awakeness. Neither state is superior. There are no such things as "superior" or "inferior."

Either way, there is *only* Awakeness, and you are IT *regardless* of whether you are conscious of it or not.

This very This—precisely as it *already is*—is IT.

We could say that *This*—consciousness—is not *other* than You, but certainly This does not *equal* You.

You don't even need This, but this Oneness experience desperately needs You.

127. The very nature of relativity-ness itself is the *apparent* movement from one polarity to the other. There is no such thing as a one-ended stick just as there is no such thing as a neutral experience. Neutral and experience effectively cancel each other out.

This is not to *deny* that there is such a state of neutrality; there most certainly *is*. However, it's an authorless apparent happening that happens to *no one*.

128. There is nothing *other than* Void that could come to "know" the Void.

129. Close your eyes and notice the dark field. There may be some rogue photons, but the dark field replaces everything else, does it not?

Pay close attention here, and check something out. Does the field, *this* field of your present experience, feel *dead?* Is it devoid of life? Or does it feel *dynamic?*

Can you pick up on the undercurrent of some indescribable yet undeniable sense of *aliveness*?

Isn't it the same as the sense of aliveness, *this very sense of present existence*, that's noticing Itself? *This* sense of existence right here and now? It's not "something else's" aliveness, and it's not somewhere else or some other time—there *is no* "something else right here, right now!"

We're speaking of *your* presence. You are not inert space. There is only Life and thus only *one* alive space: *this* one!

You *are* the alive space that holds that unit, and everything else, within it. Notice there is no "outside" of it, so "within" is just a convenience in languaging.

It's precisely the other way. You are the alive space holding that otherwise lifeless cadaver. It's not the space that's dead; it's the human form. These bodies are *born* dead! You are the animating presence that makes them *appear* alive.

130. Without an entity, there is no center to the dark field. There is only a sense of *being*, of presence-*ing*, of "here-*ing*." The *sense* of a central and localized "me" is easy to imagine and easy to believe, but it is never locatable and never actually confirmed.

131. What we refer to as "Void" is not a "something" that is "somewhere." It is instead a timeless *absence* of space that cannot be found. While It is the womb from which space and time are born, It, in Itself, is Unborn. It neither gains nor loses anything from any appearance or disappearance.

132. Can you find an owner of this evident and undeniable, present sense of being?

Does a *sense* of something *necessarily* point to the *truth* of anything?
Does a present *sense* of being prove there is *actual* being?

We sometimes refer to "beingness" as if it's a noun, a hard *something*.
I once thought "Betsy" was a noun. I thought it meant something *tangible*.

I have since come to see that there is no such thing as a "Betsy," although I use that word lovingly when I refer to the *unconnected* yet symbiotic patterns of Betsy-ness:

Cerebral
Cardiovascular
Respiratory

Beauty
Kindness
Love

DNA
RNA
ATP

Intelligence
Grace
Empathy

The patterns of Betsy-ness do not point to a *being*, a *center*, or a *thing*. They are apparent *attributes* devoid of a central essence.

133. Experience happens only within relativity-ness, which is itself an imaginary dream state. *Apparent* phenomena are reliant upon comparisons within the illusion of separation, meaning that there is—*apparently*—a "this" and "that," a "here" and "there," and a "me" and "other."

134. Does this *feeling* of existence positively declare that you are either *a* being or *the* being, or is it a false reference, a misstatement about what we *really* know? There *is* a sense of being. This sense of being is a truism. Notice: that much is true. But isn't that *all* we can say with any real conviction?

135. Is the *sense* of something the same thing as the *truth* of something? You have a sense of individuality. You have a sense of separation.
But does that make the implication true, that you *are* a separate individual?

Regardless of how it feels, you are *not* a *thing*.
Feel *This*.
Sense your unnamable, invisible, *indivisible Self*, your unbounded vastness.
You have no innate qualities, yet you are the *potential* for *all* qualities, all objects, all thought.
This Self is prior to time; it comes before all stories, even the story of "I am." It is prior to space.

You are *That Which Is*, before, during, and after any Big Bang, which is widely rumored to be the "Beginning." There *IS NO BEGINNING!*

136. Notice that there is a sense of existence, a simple sense of consciousness.

Can you locate it?
Can you measure it?
Does it have a center?
An edge?
Any boundary?
Where does it stop?
Does it stop?

137. We make a presumption that someone, an "I," *has* this sense of being, that somewhere it has an *owner.* Is that true? Can you *find* an owner, or is there just a *sense* of one?

Can anyone or anything genuinely lay claim to the sense of being? There is certainly that implication hanging in the air. Is the *implication* of something the same thing as the *truth* of something? This phenomenon is known in linguistic and philosophical communities as a *false* implication. Something is implied, but there's nothing to back it up.

When we look for that so-called "owner" we are

confronted with the fact that we simply can't *find* one. Can we absolutely, positively state who, what, or even *that* we are?

Based on our present experience, isn't it true that we can only report on the fact that there is a *sense* of existence, a *sense* of being?

138. This *immediate* sense of existence allows for the feeling *that* you are. Does it in any way imply *what* you are? Tell yourself the truth: do you know what "you" are?

139. There is a *sense* of undulation or underlying movement.

You are That which is prior to all existence-*ing*; prior to be*ing*; prior to think*ing*, experienc*ing*, or know*ing*.

There is no birth-*ing* for you, hence no death-*ing*. There is only Life-*ing:* forever unborn, unbound, and untouched.

140. All apparent looking arises *from* the same Source, but *through* different sensing devices, by which I mean the various body-mind units we typically *believe* we are.

Believe it not, we are *not* what we *believe* we are. There is a sense of thing-ness, but there is no-thing.

Instead, we are what we come to *Know* we are during the awakening and clearing process. Truth is uncovered by no one, for no one, and is seen to be already shining.

Most of human life is like watching a football game from the bleachers and believing you are on the field and in the game. There is tension, sweat, excitement, fear, and joy, but you will never win a trophy.

141. It's not a "Fred" who has "got" this sense of being; it's the sense of being that births Oneness, and it is this Oneness which apparently births Fredness. There cannot be the subset of *"the sense of being a Fred"* until there is first the raw, impersonal *sense of being* to act as its foundation.

The sense of being is more primal than "I am." "I am" is

the saloon door "between" nonduality and duality. The sense of being *is* nonduality, although the norm is that nonduality is constantly experienced but only rarely recognized—by itself!

142. There is only the One "substance," if we can call IT that. Yet IT reflects differently by way of, and through, disparate conditioning. Call it a trick of light, just as a rainbow is a trick of light. This *trick* is how Oneness *appears* as discrete things within Wholeness.

There are many illusions, but only the One Truth.

Stepping yet further back, we can see that even Oneness is an arising, something that comes and goes.

Test it. What do you really remember before that unit's birth? There is *zero* recall *here*.

To *what* does the Oneness experience appear and disappear?

143. This world is not other than you. But it is not *equal* to you.

You cannot *look* at anything and say, "There I *am*."

Similarly, you cannot look at anything and say, "There I am *not*."

144. The Void is a timeless *absence* of space. It is the womb from which space and time are born. It neither gains nor loses anything from any apparent appearance or disappearance.

145. The term "Void" is a *pointer.* Only.
Void is not a description of "something else." There *is* nothing else.
In fact, in truth, there is only No-thing, which is beyond existing and not existing.

146. Awakening may give rise to the feeling that you may lose your beloved, the all-important personal character who is believed to have been running things.

But you are *not* that character; there is no *actual* character! You are Awakeness. And you, Awakeness, are presently experiencing what it would be like if you *were* a particular character!

That body is your "portal" that leads you into the virtual reality of "I *am*, the Universe *is*, and experiencing involves intention and free agency." There is nothing in this dream that you can gain or lose, because there is nothing to this dream.

It's not even *your* dream!

The "personal me" you believe yourself to be is being dreamed by That-which-knows-no-separation.

147. *Life-ing* is an experience that contains an upside and a downside, a "this" and a "that." There is no means of experien*cing* without both. There has to be a sense of *contrast* before experiencing can arise.

Hence, all movement occurs *upon* the background of stillness. You are the *potential* for the "background world" upon which "your" character and those "you" love and hate make their appearances. You, Awakeness, are the screen upon which all characters appear.

You are also the "foreground," as well as That into which all appearances disappear.

148. What we typically term "Void" is True Reality Itself. It is That empty fullness *from which* all manifestation arises and into which all manifestation falls.

149. Void is *That* which we relentlessly try, yet always fail, to accurately speak about at retreats, in satsang, or through videos and podcasts.

We also fail to write *about* IT (accurately) in books like this one.

When it is realized that there is only IT, there is no one to read or write or say anything *about* IT. But we soon discover that the *attempts* to do so are sublime.

150. This is *IT*, and there is only *this* This, no other.

The present expression, "*this* This", is unfolding from That which can never be *known* but which is, in fact, what You always already *are*.

151. For the sake of languaging-to-be-helpful, as opposed to absolute accuracy, let us call That-which-is-prior-to-consciousness *"No-thing,"* meaning it is beyond being a thing or *not* being a thing, beyond birth, life, and death.

No-thing is Truth Itself. Whatever that is.

It never wavers, never changes, and never moves. IT is prior to the appearance of relative polarities. We can know *of* IT, but we cannot directly come to *know* IT because there is *only* IT.

Consciousness cannot *know* That which is prior to consciousness.
Whatever That *is*, You *are* That.

152. There is nothing *other* than Void which could come to *know* the Void.

153. That core primal identification with the body, with its instincts such as hunger, thirst, and a *sense* of individuality, does not entirely disappear upon awakening. It is "practical programming"; it is useful within the relative world.

It is not Your enemy. You don't have any enemies. How could you when there is nothing *other* than You? Are You your own enemy?

We don't need it to go away, and the unit would wither if it did.

You are unconscious awakeness become Conscious Awakeness, and all experience is open to you. You need only recognize that you know that you are not *only* the person, the thoughts, or the body.

We cannot truthfully say either that you are or are not that body, because we cannot truthfully report that there even *is* a body.

You are the *one thing going on*, which *includes* the appearance of that body and its thoughts.

154. We are all looking *from* the same Source, but *through* different sensing devices.

155. Whatever it is that *believes* it is a character that oh-so-desperately wants to *"get it,"* already *is* IT.

156. You are beyond "Am" and "Am not."

However, You don't *know* Yourself prior to consciousness. The sense of being, of aliveness, is the birth of undifferentiated consciousness.

When the sense "I am" arises from the *feeling of being,* it marks the apparent birth of the experience of duality.

There *is no* duality.

157. We tend to focus on the Jack-o-lanterns, but nonduality is not about pumpkins; it's about the candle, and the light that shines *through* the Jack-o-lantern.

"Lovely" or "ugly," "good" or bad" are all false, comparative, dualistic labels that occur within the living perfection of *Oneness-without-contrast.*

We are a species of pumpkin-watchers who care little about light, but who hold specific pumpkins in high regard while standing in the dark.

158. The character-unit is a construct that includes the genetic, mental, and emotional conditioning playing out, through a body and a brain.

159. Is there a "you" here plus Oneness "over there"? I'm suggesting that there is no "over there" there.

160. *You* are the presence which animates the corpse that you *think* you are, and more, much more. Or perhaps I should say that you are less, much less. There is much less going on here than meets the eye.

You undersell yourself. You are not merely an empty vessel; you are also the beneficial space "within" the vessel and the benevolent spaciousness "outside" of it.

161. There is no personal anything. In fact, there is not anything at all, *period!* Thus, there is only Noneness apparently arising as Oneness.

And Oneness is simply the experienc*ing* of "thing-ness" by *No*-thing.

162. There is only Oneness and nothing but Oneness. You declare that you understand this truth intellectually, but that it is *not* your experience?

If what you are saying is true, then is that not *Oneness* grumbling to *Oneness* that *Oneness* is not having the "*Oneness* experience"? Is that even possible?

163. Recognize that Truth is far, far beyond what a three-pound brain can conceive.

164. There is no viewpoint until we believe we are a separate being, with a limited, focused field. Prior to that belief there is only a view*port*. Look *through* that body instead of *as* that body.

165. That which cannot be described looks upon that which can be described, just as the unmanifest comes to experience itself as the manifest.

166. What you're looking *from* is what you're looking *for*.

The seeker is the sought; the dog has been chasing its tail.

Welcome to the Cosmic Joke.

167. Once we see what we are not, we see that Truth has always, already, been shining. "We" awaken. But *what is it* that awakens?

The "character" or ego (patterns working symbiotically with each other) often assumes that it will be the one to experience this sublime event. But awakening only happens when the character steps aside. You, not the character, awaken. Awakeness itself awakens.

168. Between 1992, when I had my first awakening experience, and 2006, when this present awakening first began, I thought I knew the truth. What I didn't realize is that the one who thought it knew the truth did not exist.

169. What is that unit's looking *tool*? If you're looking for that unit's socks or its keys or its True Nature, what do you use to look for it?
What is your *looking device*?

Is it not *attention*?
Attention is your looking tool, yes?

Of course.
Always.

Having seen this, would you agree that a decent definition of attention might be *focused awareness*?

Has attention been looking for something *outside* of Awareness? Can you currently find anything *outside* of Awareness?
Could you ever find anything *outside* of Awareness?
How many *awareness*es do you count?

170. How long do you think Awareness could *look for* Awareness?

171. The eyes that are reading this sentence cannot see themselves. At best, they can only occasionally see a *reflection*.

172. The belief that there was someone who once had something wonderful and mysterious but had consequently lost it and was now desperately seeking to get it back, was the only thing stopping Awakeness from noticing its always-already-present nature.

173. The *unquestioned belief* in a seeker who will one day become liberated is itself the only obstruction to noticing that there is no seeker and hence, there can be no bondage or liberation.

174. Awakeness-in-disguise is *pretending* to be bound so that it can *pretend* to be a seeker who will one day *soon* become a finder.

175. Take a moment and go back to what you remember as your "previous" awakening experience. Get that scene in your head as clearly as you can.
Now, tell me, *who was it* that woke up?

176. From the absolute view, there is nothing to be gained from awakening. Only an ego can clamor for "more" or "other."

177. Before the so-called awakening happened here, I

was pinning all of my hopes on an imaginary character. Let's look at the logic of that.

An imaginary bowl cannot hold water any more than imaginary water can wash a bowl. In that same vein, it is impossible for a make-believe character ever to have an awakening.

Fred desperately wanted to awaken to the truth of God. Instead, what happened was that God woke up to the fiction of Fred.

178. In the absence of the character, is there any desire for more, or for something other than this? This character is not living; it is *being lived*.

179. In the absence of a character, what is it that has to wake up?
Awakeness wakes up to Awakeness. It awakens to Itself.

180. Previously, "my" attention was looking for awareness, but then I recognized that attention *is* alert Awareness.
Who noticed this?
No one.

Attention simply started paying attention *to* attention. That changed the fundamental nature of "my" experience.

181. Everywhere I look—above or below, forward or backward, right or left—I see only the Face of God.

182. When everything else disappears, what is left?

183. You think you're a Susan or a Bob, because there's a *sense* that you're a Susan or a Bob.

Is a *sense* of something the same thing as the *truth* of something?
(I had a sense that it was going to rain here today. It *didn't*.)

Upon awakening, we come to see there is no Susan and no Bob.

Given that we have already seen that there is no Susan or Bob, what chance do you think I have of waking up these fictional characters?

Since neither the Susan character nor the Bob character ever woke up to begin with, what are the odds of my waking either one up *again*?

Since the character-unit doesn't wake up when awakening occurs, what *does* wake up?

What is here, that is *not* a Susan or a Bob, that has previously *believed* it was a Susan or a Bob?

184. What you're looking *with* (attention) is what you're looking *for* (awareness.)

185. There is no such thing as "Got it!" because there is no one to *get* it—or *keep* it, or *lose* it and get it back. There is just *Getting it right now.*

186. There is *only* This-Here-Now.
There is absolutely *nothing* else.
Ever.

187. As with everything else I say, it is not *true.* But it is *effectively* true, and we don't suffer from technicalities.

The patterns that naturally come together symbiotically

to formulate character*ness* are essentially *programmed* to invent, believe in, and identify with a nonexistent character. Therefore, "the make-believe character" cannot ever come to know or accept that there *is no character.*

Nothing changes until *Awakeness* recognizes this endless loop. When Awakeness comes to experience itself consciously, there is an immediate 180-degree shift in perception. This perceptual shift is something that cannot be anticipated or understood.

188. Outside of imagination, there are no options afforded by What Is.
There are no alternatives, and there is no comparison to This-Here-Now, because there is *only* This-Here-Now.

189. *When* does awakening happen?

Where does awakening happen?

To *what* does awakening happen?

190. Our "inheritance teachings" have always told us and sold us on the so-called "sure fact" that we must surrender to the absolute. My question is, "*To whom do they refer?*"

191. It may *feel like* there is "someone" who is surrendering or who has surrendered to God. That's typically what a character will claim, which is wholly understandable.

Fredness felt that way, too. Often, even in post-awakening.

However, the *feeling* of something is not the same thing as the *truth* of something. So, this feeling of "personal surrender" is not ultimately true. In fact, it is an *impossibility*, because there is no "personal me" here to "personally surrender."

There's no one home to do it, keep it, or lose it. The lights are on, but the house is empty. Surrender simply *is* until it isn't. It's not the imaginary individual who surrenders to God. It's just the opposite.

It's God, so to speak, who unconditionally surrenders

to the experiencing of an imaginary individual in an illusory world.

192. The so-called "surrendered state" cannot be forced, denied, or even *experienced* by a "separate me."

193. What is this awakening? It is the seemingly evidential event-cum-process of divinity waking up to itself and having the grand hallucination of relativity-ness.

The character can find nothing right about it, and Awakeness can find nothing wrong. Regardless of content, it is *always* the Divine experiencing the Divine.

194. Some clearing can and usually does occur prior to awakening. A seeker apparently acquiring context *about* nondual truth is a normal part of the pre-awakening process. It counts, and it's a good thing *unless* we begin to think that units really know something.

This "I think I know something now!" will remain as the hidden saboteur for the rest of that unit's life.

195. Awakening sometimes occurs through those who have sought it or even have thought about it. Spontaneous awakening is not exceedingly rare but experiencing significant duration after such an experience while remaining unaided is *very* rare indeed.

I work with these people on a quite regular basis. Seeing the truth is one thing. *Being* truth is quite another.

196. Surrender *happens* by itself. No one *does* it. IT awakens *through* a body, although it will likely be recalled as having been an experience that happened *to* a unit-character.

Having thoroughly *seen through* the imaginary character, Awakeness comes to accept the unit, its conditioning, its circumstances, and all of apparent manifestation absolutely and unconditionally. Stories mean nothing to Awakeness, nor do they have any effect upon it.

While it is true that Awakeness "lives" beyond space and time, look where the *unit* is "living"—right in the *middle* of space and time. Therefore, there is always an experience of time *by the character* as Awakeness pulls free of the web it has been dreaming.

In this Teaching we call that experience "clearing." We don't attempt to clear the character *up*; we work on clearing the *sense* of a character *out*. We appear to do this through nondual inquiry, but in truth it simply happens while we appear to be doing something.

I do not *really* understand anything about awakening. No one does.

197. The character cannot have an awakening experience, because awakening is recognizing the *unreality* of the character. There is a *role* that remains, but there is no player to fill it.

198. Some say liberation is the embracing of the now, but here it seems to be more like the recognition of This-Here-Now by This-Here-Now, followed by divine acceptance.

199. Any memory of an awakened state or experience "belongs" to the character only.

Wholly illusory patterns claim to be the creator, discoverer, master, or victim of wholly illusory patterns.

200. We are consciously awake to this experience—or not. Either way is 100% fine. It is only the make-believe character that posits that it would like to be—and indeed *should* be—alert to True Nature at all times.

201. Awakeness is as it is, and that's *all* there is. There is only the truth, which is singular—there *is no comparison* to it. In the absence of an imagined contrast, can you find a problem here?

202. The make-believe "personal me" cannot "wake up" or have that dramatic spiritual insight for which we have always longed. Only *Awakeness* can "wake up", meaning that only *Awakeness* can come to see and acknowledge that there *is no "personal me."*

203. In the absence of that unit-character's opinion, how's your day going?

204. When Truth unveils Itself *to* Itself, Awakeness comes to see that in the absence of a "separate me", there is only This–*exactly as it already is.* We need to see both what we are *not* (the character) and what we *are* (Awakeness).

205. The only way to get the so-called "separate me"

out of our way is to see that there was never an "individual me" present to begin with. It's not Fred who recognizes that there is no Fred; it's Awakeness that comes to see that there is no Fred.

206. The character is wholly imaginary. Given that it is illusory, this imaginary character can *never* wake up, gain weight, be tamed, or eat a sandwich.

207. When we are in the Bubble of Self-Reflection, only Awakeness can see through it. This seems to be quite straightforward, because there is nothing there to see through. But we don't know there is nothing there until there is an actual experiencing of the absence of the character.

No-thing comes to see that there is No-thing there.

208. If you had to prove to me, right at this moment, that you are *not* awake, could you do it?

209. This conscious experiencing of True Nature is not a "spiritual experience"; it's just Awakeness coming out of denial. In my 12-step work, I used to help pull drunks out of denial. Now I—Awakeness itself—via a staged play so intricate that it would embarrass all of Broadway, appears to pull Awakeness out of denial.

Awakeness pretends to be asleep, so that it can pretend to be awakened.

Go figure.

210. It's so simple, you could miss it—*and we usually do.*
It is always here and always clear.

It is This, and This is You, yet This is not all of You.
You can do without This, but This cannot exist without You.

There is No-thing before This, and there is No-thing after This.
You are This *and* That, yet there is no separation.

You are Not-Two.

211. *What is it* that declares, "I am not awake?"
What is it that declares, "I should be?"

212. Given that Oneness and *only* Oneness exists, then *what is it* that is telling Oneness that it is "separate" from Oneness and that it's not having the Oneness "experience?"

213. The one who wants to break free of the imagined character *is* the imagined character. There is no true liberation, because there is no true bondage. Bondage is only for the *imagined* character.

214. You *are* the very Awakeness that you seek. The dog is chasing its tail.

How long do you think a dog could chase its tail without catching it?

215. "Awakening" is when Awakeness comes to notice *itself*, when attention notices attention, when the field of awareness recognizes the field of awareness.

216. Awakening without clearing is like the sun rising without shining.

217. No "individual" can correctly "recall" the fullness of an awakening event, because if the event was authentic, then no character was present to remember it. Awakeness never shows up in the character's *presence*, but only in the character's *absence*.

218. What we refer to as that "magical moment of clarity" is simply the cessation of identification as a character. It's not so much a happening as it is an *un*happening.

219. There is just *one* authentic awakening, which is the process of Awakeness supposedly "awakening" to (*noticing*) the fact that it is Awakeness itself and that there is no *other*, including the *apparently* perceiving unit.

Further noticing, which this Teaching calls "clearing," reveals that Awakeness is *apparently* expressing itself as the content of this dream moment, as experienced through this dream body, within this wholly illusory world.

220. We *are* the awake space that we believe we have been living *in*. We are not experiencing "it"; IT is experiencing "us."

221. The willingness and ability to *hear* the truth when you are presented with it is normally essential for awakening to occur. However, the choice to hear the truth is not made by "you," because there is no "you" to make that choice or not.

It happens, or it doesn't. It is all Oneness' call.

222. All of us expect conscious Awakeness to show up in our presence objectively. We want to know what it feels like to be in the presence of conscious Awakeness. But conscious Awakeness can only arise in our *absence* (in the absence of the make-believe character you think you are); it cannot arise in our *presence*.

223. The unit that you think you *are* is just another object within the space that you think you are *in*. It is not the center of this world. There is *no* center anywhere. There is nothing to be equidistant *from*.

There is just "*here*," whatever that means.

Seeing *thisness* as This and This as *thisness* is effectively understanding the Math of One.

224. Completely counter-intuitively, space is not *partitioning* everything *from* "everything else"; it's what's *holding* everything together instead. Space is not the great *partitioner*; it's the great *uniter*.

Right now, trade space for form. *Right now*, stop and move space to the foreground of this arising instead of imagining it as the background. Don't just *read* this; *do the exercise!*

Then you, Oneness, can come to consciously *see/be* Oneness As It Is.

225. Realizing *whose* experience it is—*that* is awakening.

226. Look around that room and notice the objects. That should be easy; it's what you've done all of your life.

Now, look again around that same area. This time, focus on the space around and behind those objects instead of on the objects themselves. Notice what's already there: an "invisible absence."

Now, imagine that same spaciousness as pudding. How many puddings do you count?

227. Note that after "your" awakening, it becomes clear that it was *not* "your" awakening! There is no individual left to bask in the glow of its own wisdom.

It is always *Awakeness'* awakening, always for its own purposes or lack of purposes. It is not meant to elevate or inform an imaginary character, even though it usually leaves that feeling *in its wake.*

228. To awaken, you must be willing to admit that you are a failure as an independent entity.

Evidently, the vast majority would rather die in denial of that fact, rather than in the freedom of Awakening. It has always been so.

229. Be fully open to what you *don't* know. If what you knew worked, you'd already be free.

230. The ideal way for you to wake up is precisely the way that you do wake up. *You can't get it wrong.*

In that same way, how you are *clearing up* is also perfect—for that particular sack of conditioning. The process begins by disavowing ownership of what may be translated by the mind as "your" experience, and it unfolds exactly as it must.

231. A *sense* of "individual surrender" arises when we "agree to accept" what is already going on anyway. We "give God the go-ahead" to be What Is As It Is, which has always already been the case *anyway.*

However, surrender in this minimal measure is ultimately *mandatory.* The body and its world already have to do what they do; there is just an also-inevitable cessation of the mind attempting to do otherwise. That is merely unresisted Self-recognition.

232. Rather counter-intuitively, Awakeness *includes* experiences of cloudiness. That is just as it should be. To resist What Is As It Is Right Now is the surest way to hasten and then prolong cloudiness. Even though there's no one *doing* the resisting, such will be the nature of the experience.

Awakeness is always here and always clear. It does not require assistance from a character. However, the sack of conditioning it appears to be pouring through in the dream is neither of those.

Ever.

233. There will be a belief in an "individual's" free will until the believer of that illusion is seen through.

After all, that conditioning is the very basis for relativity-ness, which seems to be true, *but isn't.*

234. Awakening is not something we *do*; it is something that we *stop* doing.

235. There is Oneness and *only* Oneness. Given this truth, *what is it* that can experience a sense of individuality?

236. We think of post-awakening as being the

disappearance of "individual resistance," through what *appears* to be a process of gradual acceptance over time.

There is no individual to begin with, so this can't possibly be the case. What's really happening is that the deep sense of individuality and the sense of an individual *managing its life* disappear instead. *It ends when it ends*—no sooner, no later. We can't stop it, and we can't rush it. Everything is on full automation.

Contrary to what we have always been deeply concerned about, the body does not then proceed to run amok. We don't end up being killers or homeless pushers of grocery carts. We can only *be what we are*, which is devoid of either action or consequence.

237. Relativity-ness, which is entirely dependent upon contrast, cannot, by its very nature, surrender to Awakeness. It simply does what it does.

Ultimately the only surrender that can happen is when Awakeness surrenders to relativity-ness. IT simply is what It Is.

238. The vast field of awareness is unfocused. Attention, we can note, is *focused* consciousness, consciousness-in-action. Attention arises simultaneously with a false sense of limited identity. That's why we refer to it as "my" attention or "her" attention.

This incorrect identification brings about an experience of the apparent *contraction of the Infinite.* Remember, *any* identification—even as Oneness—is claiming that there is *something* when in fact there isn't any-thing.

239. There is a *sense* of individuality, and there is the unit's experience of *feeling* like an individual, but there is no genuinely discrete entity of any kind. That which senses itself as an individual *is not* separate.

240. Waking up is not a process of *addition*; it's a process of *subtraction.* When we see through what *isn't* true, there's nothing left to do.

Unhindered, Truth naturally shines by Itself.

241. Like the *sense* of individuality with which it goes hand-in-glove, attention is Infinity experiencing a *sense* of itself as an imaginary distinct, separate being with a particular, limited, localized vantage point. Playing our part of the role in this dream, "we" then invent a *name* for this imaginary being and attach that name to an animated corpse through which raw attention operates, finally declaring that said object has "free will" and that it is *us*.

242. Nondual inquiry means we question *everything* down to the roots. We cease to take anything "known" for granted. We investigate *every* assumption, no matter how long we have held onto it. Until finally, the illusion is seen through and begins to drop away.

243. As Consciousness comes to identify with one of these units, it begins to believe in that singular view. The unit's family, friends, and community—who are also Consciousness-in-disguise—take great pains to help brainwash the new arrival.

"Hi, Bob." "Bye, Bob." "Do *this*, Bob." "Don't do *that*, Bob."

In this way, *Consciousness trains Consciousness* to believe it is just one particular unit.

244. Confession is a tried-and-true accelerant of clarity. Just tell yourself the truth for a change, Awakeness. This dream was fun until it wasn't. We cannot both pledge allegiance to an *idea* and expect to be beacons of clarity.

245. When we come to recognize True Nature, the "consciousness camera" that believed it was facing outward *from* the unit begins to "pan back," so that the view now *includes* the unit.

There is no other actual "viewpoint" than this. It doesn't belong to anyone. I think of it as a view *porthole*, which is also false, but I find that term to be more helpful. Instead of looking *for* Awakeness, we can more easily see that we are always already looking *from* Awakeness.

246. Awakening to True Nature happens when we somehow "become willing" to question deeply our most core assumptions, all of the things we think we know so well. However, awakening occurs not as a result of what we *know*. Rather, it comes via the happy *unknowing* of everything we thought we knew so well.

Drop the pretense of having knowledge, and Truth will appear in its place. However, this "Knowledge of Truth" is of an entirely different order than that to which we are accustomed.

It is closer to *grokking* it, but even that doesn't really say it either.

247. Nondual inquiry is not a search for truth. It is Truth in search of the bottommost lie that this illusion is built upon.

And no, it is never "over." Who would it be over *for*?

248. *Inquiry is not about finding an answer; it is about finding the questioner, or rather, discovering the pause that occurs when the mind stops in response to the questions. Here are a few common examples:*

Is there really a "Fred Davis?"
Who's asking?

Is this *my* body, *my* house, *my* life?
Who wants to know?

Are these thoughts really *my* thoughts?
Can you <u>locate</u> whoever is referred to by this "my"?

Do I have to *believe* these thoughts?
What is the origin of these thoughts?

When everything drops away, what remains?
*What has *always* been here that you simply haven't noticed?*

Now let go of even *that.*

249. Immediately after an initial awakening, ego pops

back up, much like whack-a-mole. It's automated. You can't stop it, because *there's no you there to do so.*

250. Enlightenment requires the willingness to have the rug pulled out from underneath you.
Not just once, but over, and over, and over again.
Right now!
And now, and now, and now, and now, and now.

251. When the false mask of a "separate me" drops away, that seeing/being acts like and feels like, a *real* hammer has slammed down and successfully obliterated the ego once and for all.

To our utter amazement, that seeing/being is not the "end" of anything *for* somebody. It's almost always the *beginning* of a long game of whack-a-mole.

The duration and depth of suffering experienced in the clearing process can be modified—but not by "you"!

252. The belief, "I am not awake," always *feels* true, but it never *is* true.

253. Immediately following awakening, the unit-character will exclaim, "Wow! I have it now! I could *never* 'unsee' this!"

But that is a lie. In fact, it is the *character's* lie, and its very utterance is conclusive evidence that the glimpse of Truth has *already* been "unseen."

254. When Truth is finally recognized, what we see is that there is not now, and never has there been, a Fred, Betsy, Bob, or Barbara. There is no *actual* "personal me" that can be found somewhere within the vague *sense* of a "personal me."

Tornadoes are pilotless and represent the potential for tragedy. And so it is for these human units as well.

255. Student: "I'm awake! What do I do *now*?"

Fred: "You are *not* awake; you are Awake*ness*.

And Awakeness, I suggest you continue 'doing' the same thing you were 'doing' before awakening."

Student: "What's that?"

Fred: "*Nothing.*"

256. Thoughts arise spontaneously in response to conditions.
Human beings are hardwired to believe them.

The vital question is, "Are we *required* to believe them?" Of course, the answer is "No," but strangely we will believe them *anyway*, due to the wiring.

Human beings are also hooked up to believe that they are *personally* thinking the automated, condition-sponsored thoughts that arise within What Is.

Nondual inquiry is the only active defense against these automated beliefs. It is the only path I know that has a *direct* correlation with awakening.

Other practices can be helpful, healthy, and excellent for calming the mind and soothing the body. But nothing else I know of has the built-in power of nondual inquiry to *free* us. *Nothing.*

257. Our imaginary character cannot free our *imaginary character.* This is an endless loop. Nor can I possibly "wake up" *that which is not real to begin with.*

258. The essential mechanism of the dream is the appearance of cause and effect. All apparent activity or arising within *relativity-ness* is purely a matter of latent conditioning "magnetically" rising to meet circumstance.

There is neither plan nor planner; things happen because they *can't not* happen. Anything beyond that is story. No thought is true, *including* the ones that say:

"I am now *permanently* awake."

"I am *completely* awake!"

"I am *not* awake."

"I *used* to be awake."

"I'm *going to* wake up—*soon!*"

"I'm on the *edge* of enlightenment!"

"I *understand* nonduality."

"Oneness is *not* my experience."

"I'm only missing *one little piece.*"

"I used to be clear, but now I am cloudy."

Those statements are not just *false*; they are 180 degrees away from even the *beginning* of an ending.

259. There is never more than the pilotless *sense* of a "personal me". When we try to track it down, it never seems to be where we are looking! It is absolutely *unlocatable.* This is not just a so-called "individual" experience; it is the universal experience of *individuality*—for *Oneness!*

260. Many of the people I work with every day are smarter than I am. There is, however, one thing that I know that virtually none of them do, and that is the Math of One.

I have taught it to physicists, philosophers, and PhDs of every stripe. It's really quite simple; it's just nearly always overlooked. The Math of One states unequivocally that "*one* equals *one.*" There is Oneness and only Oneness. There is nothing "outside" or "other" than Oneness that can come to see Oneness objectively and plant a flag of victory.

"*You*" have got to be Oneness. "*I*" have got to be Oneness. In fact, THIS, whatever it is, *has got to be* IT! And yes, I'm referring to *this* very This! There is only Oneness and nothing *but* Oneness.

So tell me, Oneness, have you been waiting for the "*other*" Oneness to show up?

261. Awakening is less of a *seeing* and more of a seeing *through.* We see through the "invisible veil" that is *rumored* to surround Truth.

Nothing "surrounds" Truth. There is *only* Truth, and You are It.

262. Incredibly, upon awakening, the first thing we find out about bondage is that there isn't any! There never has been! Must we strive to free what's already free or just help Freedom Itself notice that it is Freedom Itself?

263. Waking up is coming to see that waking up is not only unnecessary; it's *impossible!*

264. Waking up is "seeing" that there's only This; there is no character which can wake up. Clearing up is accepting there is only This *As It Is*.

265. Within moments after "enlightenment" has *appeared* to occur through a given unit, most egos will snap back and begin to rebuild.

The first building block of rebuilding the ego is the hijacking of an awakening that no one had, at which point ego is made happy. "Oh my God! *I* finally got it!" Ego now declares that *it* woke up instead of IT. The belief is that there is someone "back home" in the body which now knows the big secret of nonduality.

In truth, this self-proclaimed "true seeing" is just another self-centered corruption of presently *being* True Nature.

We cannot ever "see" our True Nature objectively, but there's no object involved—only an *implied* subject. Nothing objective can ever be "real," if our definition of "real" is like Ramana Maharshi's.

"The world is illusory,
Only Brahman is real,
Brahman is the world."

266. With initial awakening, we "see" something that

we can't completely "unsee." Yet we can and usually do forget what it was that we "saw," which is sometimes worse than not seeing IT at all.

Now, instead of just being an ordinary seeker, we grant ourselves the bogus status of being an "elevated seeker." In fact, we are simply frustrated *re-seekers*.

267. Through awakening, Oneness comes to see through the illusion of the existence of a "personal me." The best it can do is see what it is *not*. Oneness cannot see itself any more than an eye can see itself.

268. "Going cloudy" is when the patterns that "form" a formless ego move in and heavily filter or block Truth from Itself, like a cloud that has settled in front of the sun. As soon as the cloudiness is recognized as cloudiness, ego then attempts to "once again" initiate an amazingly special and wonderful awakening *it never experienced to begin with!*

Seekers are waiting for Truth to unveil Itself to a seeker. That has never, ever happened to anyone, at any time, and it never will.

Truth arises in the conscious absence of a seeker and unveils Itself to Itself.

269. Clearing is not about clearing anyone *up*; it's about clearing residual conditioning *out*! Stated more accurately, it's the *thinning* of "character-ness," the gradual diminution of resistance to What Already Is.

270. The experienced-but-nonetheless-unreal "personal me" does not and cannot come to see Oneness—there *is* no "personal me". *What isn't* cannot come to see What Is. What Is notices what isn't instead.

We have to recognize over and over again that Reality works *backward* from the way unit-characters think it does.

271. Awakening is an *invitation*, not a *graduation*. It's an invitation *to* the dance, but it is *not* the dance itself.

The dance is the apparent process of our "clearing" within post-awakening.

It is a very different sort of clearing than what we normally refer to. We're simply clearing out all of the stuff we think we know, when in fact we don't know anything at all. Thank goodness!

272. The unawakened mind (so to speak!) will assume that the imaginary character which Awakeness has always believed itself to be is the one who will be first waking up and then clearing up. This common notion is utterly false.

Instead, initial awakening is coming to see that there *is no imaginary character to wake up*! There is only Awakeness, be it conscious or unconscious (of Itself). Given that there *is no* imaginary character, we have to surrender the concept of a "personal me", knowing that we can't wake up or clear up what was never present to begin with.

273. Units do what units do. Maya is always in full swing.

274. What's present in the centerless space, in the very same space that we always hallucinated *we were the center of*, is merely sets of *patterns*. They are unowned, unmanaged, fully automated energetic patterns. In this Teaching, I refer to those patterns as *unit conditioning*.

Unit conditioning is the inherited patterns contained in DNA combined with the environmental patterns which have been overlaid subsequent to the birth of the unit. We usually refer to it as "nature and nurture."

275. When unit conditioning reacts to external events at a subconscious level, I term it *"conditioned reflex."* It is a symbiotic coalition of patterns arising from both nature and nurture, as well as the local conditions in which they have emerged.

In full-blown post-awakening, units continue to function through blind patterns (meaning that there are *only* patterns), often in foolish and/or unskillful ways. This is vexing, until it's not.

Awakeness can instead recognize that it has *no power over* relativity-ness. Oneness happens as it does. There is neither alternative nor comparison. At that point, we can see that ultimately, Awakeness has to surrender to relativity-ness.

276. Prior to awakening, we thought we would find Oneness expressing itself as all-goodness-perfection-without-end. We woke up and discovered that *in the absence of contrast, no experiencing could happen.* There is no such thing as a one-ended stick.

"Good and bad" come in the same box, with a single delivery.

277. "Oneness-without-perceived-fault" is a spiritually immature concept, something akin to a generic heaven. The funny thing about Oneness is that there's just *one* of them. Thus, Oneness is, by definition, all-inclusive. It *includes* the world just as it is right now, and it necessarily encompasses all the so-called "faults" that are found in relativity-ness.

278. By its very nature, relativity-ness has to *appear* to move. A yin-yang symbol is always in apparent movement—within each extreme there lies the seed of the other extreme—and you are more like a *verb* than a *noun.*

279. We think that conscious Awakeness will someday show up in "our" *presence,* but conscious Awakeness can only show up in the character's *absence.* Awakeness wakes up from the dream of being a character.

280. The great obstacle to awakening is the *belief in an imaginary character* who someday will "wake up." But there is no one for that to happen to or not happen to. Nor is there anything more that needs to happen. There is no such thing as "more!"

281. Characters do not exist now, nor have they ever existed. Nonetheless, the "ghosts" (meaning *unowned patterning*) of millions of never-born characters are desperately trying to understand nondual reality via the intellect. This cannot occur.

Nevertheless, let us not ignore nor overlook the intellect. It is the first wave of the changing tide.

282. Waiting for someone to "find" the absence of a "someone" is an endless cycle. I term this the "Bubble of Self-Reflection." Its only usefulness is to wear out the seeker's fascination with relativity-ness.

283. When a client we'll call Susan says to me early on in an Awakening Session, "I already know there is no Susan," Susan*ness* is unintentionally lying to me. I don't take it personally.

The problem lies in the belief in a character who can

"get it" or "not get it," who "has it" or "used to have it" and then "lost it" and now desperately "wants it back."

This is all silly imagination, but it's exactly the kind of silly imagining that can and does keep us going around in the great Seeker-Circle-Cycle for decades.

It's the default position until it's not. And what eventually sees through it is neither "Bob" nor "Bobness."

284. There is only the arising of thought followed by an automated belief in it. It's *all* automated. I'm not saying, "we are robots"; I'm saying, *"we are not"*!

285. What wakes up is, of course, *Awakeness itself.* The conditioning here—i.e., the patterning that creates the illusion of personhood—does not wake up. The unit does not wake up. Neither one of them have the capacity to do so.

Awakening is, at last, seeing through the myriad patterns of Maya, "breaking free" from the illusion of being a distinct entity and noticing that there was never any bondage to begin with. This freedom is not *new*; it is just finally *realized.*

Full realization is not the same thing as *initial recognition*. It falls into the so-called "clearing process." Clarity Sessions are not about clearing "someone" *up*. They are about clearing old character patterns *out*.

286. *"Is awakening an event or a process?"*

My first response is *"Who wants to know?"* because that is the only *relevant* question.

A senior student will catch that and instantaneously clear—or they won't. Typically, they do. If I have to explain it, it's already too late. I'd be like a comedian trying to explain a great joke that went right over the audience's heads. There's no point; I just move on.

The more satisfying answer for a student will generally be that just like all the rest of nonduality, it's not either-or, it's *both*. You are not just the vastness, but you are certainly not just a human being. You're both.

Initial awakening is usually an *"event,"* which may be blissful, electrifying, or sometimes ordinary—so ordinary that the mind doesn't even record it. But it is never the *character's* "event." That's just memory, and of what use is memory to the Eternal Now?

287. We can't really talk about this. The absolute absence of a "we" contributes mightily to this.

288. *Claim* your awakening.
Claim it or "lose" it; it's just that simple.
"Claiming" allows for the complete abandonment of seeking.

289. What a so-called "unawakened" student doesn't realize when they come to me is that nearly ten times out of ten, they will have been caught in the Bubble of Self-Reflection. *Everybody* goes there—I certainly did—and almost nobody gets out of there by themselves.

In the Bubble of Self-Reflection, the one who already knows that there is no Bob—*is Bob*. That's the booby prize of nonduality.

It's only when *Awakeness* comes to see that there is no Bob that things really start happening.

290. I remember a client who lived in a 14th-century cabin in the mountains of Switzerland. Upon his awakening, he looked at me and sputtered, "You're kidding?" I shook my head to indicate that I was definitely *not* kidding! Suddenly he slapped his forehead and said, "Oh, my God! Oh, my God!"

He'd spent 30 years learning and teaching Transcendental Meditation all over the world, but all the while, he had overlooked the obvious. That's what we do. We're just "too smart" to notice the absolutely unavoidable.

We have to get a little bit *stupid* to wake up. We have to come back to Child-Mind. My job is to help very smart people get stupid enough to notice that rain is wet whether we believe it or not.

I help them confess, "Duh."

291. There are *no rules and no limitations* for God. However, there are *plenty* of people around our community who believe that there *are* lots of rules and limitations. They declare that they have the inside scoop on these, and they're happy to share the many rumors and fictitious stories they've collected over the years.

Stay away!

No one has a monopoly on Self-Realization. Run from those who say they do. And never look back!

292. Virtually everyone who reaches out to me is smart; many clients are *very* smart. After ten years of teaching, I can recall only a handful to whom that description didn't apply. Jnana Yoga is the yoga of wisdom.

However, evidence strongly points to the conclusion that intelligence apparently bears little or no relationship to *wisdom*.

This Teaching lures its students down from their ivory towers and intellectual perches. If they don't come along quietly, it will, with ever fewer exceptions, *throw* them down into the warm mud of Child-Mind.

Child-Mind is what can recognize Truth. Pure "brainiac-ing" doesn't work in this field.

293. In the first blush of awakening, we come to see that there is no "personal me." The mind-blowing part of this is that we always envisioned that the unchallenged and altogether imaginary "personal me" was someday going to finally see through the altogether imaginary "personal me" we had heard so much about.

This is a brand of such extreme, *circular lunacy* that only an *already* insane human being would even *attempt* to justify it!

294. The so-called clearing process is really the gradual *colonization* of a unit by conscious Awakeness. Within space-time, this will *look and feel like* a slow evolution. In the wake of awakening, reflexive conditioning almost always reverts to seeing through one believed thought at a time. Once in a while, you may see through a collective pocket of similar beliefs, but that's unusual.

For the unit, all of this will seem slow and plodding. Units are not famous for their patience, especially when there's no payoff for the character. One of the most common complaints I hear from those in post-awakening is, "I should be clearer than this."

It appears to be universal until it's not. Happily, Awakeness is not subject to such relative fantasies of time and space.

The character wants desperately to graduate from spirituality so it can get back to doing the fun stuff it was doing before taking this *major* wrong turn into the clutches of nonduality.

An Awakened Being has no interest in any sort of "graduation." And they wouldn't "go back" even if it was possible. The clearing process eventually becomes exquisite. It is what all spirituality is really all about. It really is about the journey, not about a goal or an endpoint.

It's about Love "coming home" to the Love that never went anywhere to begin with. I often tell people who awaken with me, "Welcome Home." It's the warmest greeting You will ever get.

295. If we are inhabiting a "lucky unit," so to speak, then through Self-realization we—by which I mean the singular *Awakeness*, of course—come to see what we are *not*. We come to see that the character we always thought we were is fictional. This "event" can happen anytime it wants, in any way it wants, through any unit it wishes to use, for its own purposes.

It sounds like I'm talking about an entity's awakening. I'm not; I'm just hamstrung by language.

296. Circular lunacy is why we unsuccessfully seek for five, ten, or even 50 years. We just can't see that we're pinning all of our hopes on the fortunes of an *imaginary character*. Given that the character is *itself* fictitious, it will *never* come to see through a make-believe character!

But that sure doesn't stop us from trying! We try until we just can't try anymore—until the suffering becomes absolutely *unbearable*, and then that unit will become a *seeking-unit*. It won't necessarily *ever* become a *finding-unit*, but it won't be from the lack of trying. And the harder we try, the less progress we make. In fact, we go backward.

How fast can an imaginary character swim? How *tall* is it? How much does it *weigh*? How much *volume* does it take up? What kind of *food* will it require? Will it ever find the perfect mate?

This leads us to the most important question of all—the only relevant question: *"Is it even possible that a made-up character could ever wake up??"*

297. Endless gradations of clarity and confusion are present within post-awakening. It's just what happens, so we must get over the idea that "I should be clearer than I am."

Says who?

Here are Fred's four Ignoble Truths:

A belief just spontaneously appeared out of thin air!
However, in the absence of inquiry, you believed it.
And now you're suffering from it.
Finally, you came to spirituality to try to overcome it.

It's as ridiculous as that. We can't STOP thinking thoughts *we* never thought to begin with! We have to consistently and skillfully question thoughts as they are noticed, hopefully as they first arise, but in any case, as fast as we can.

There is no true thought, and no thought that can withstand nondual inquiry.

298. I worked in separate sessions with two guys this past week, both of whom reported that they had awakened some years ago. They had never met each other, yet their experiences, while different, bore striking similarities.

Each believed and claimed he held a *memory* of a previous awakening. Each reported their awakening experience as having been quite blissful.

It seems that in each case, both the bliss and the clarity

had—quickly for one and very slowly for the other—either partially or wholly evaporated by the time I spoke with them. Each man felt a deep sense of loss and longing. Both desperately wanted to "get back there."

There was certainly what I call *latent wakefulness* present in each of these guys, yet they remained confused. In both cases, I could immediately tell that their stories were as *authentic* as they could relate them, even though I knew that neither one was *true*.

Interestingly, both of these guys *thought* themselves to be "clearer" than I *found* them to be. Yet both of them believed they *should be* "clearer" than either of them *considered* themselves to be. Fascinating.

Furthermore, each of them reported experiencing oscillation—the feeling of moving back and forth "into" and "out of" clarity. This so-called oscillation brought suffering in its wake.

Through skillful nondual inquiry, both joyfully "rediscovered" the secret of their awakening. These stories are not uncommon; they are the norm. They are representative of the many hundreds of stories which this teaching has influenced over the years. However, what matters most is what such stories can teach us.

You are *already* Awakeness Itself. Yet, even so, I know of no one—not a friend, nor a client, nor any teacher I'm familiar with, including *myself*—who initially experienced durable clarity and stability within the madness of Maya. Post-awakening is where the real work is. Live it or lose it.

299. Units still have preferences in post-awakening, but over what feels like "time," the need to fulfill those preferences winds down. It may sputter out altogether, I hear, but it hasn't done so here yet!

300. When awakening occurs, what "wakes up," of course, is Awakeness Itself. The conditioning—i.e., the patterning that creates the illusion of individuality—does not wake up; it has no capacity to do so. I can wake up a unit or a character exactly as well as I can wake up an empty glass or a spoon. It just ain't happening.

301. The initial unveiling of the cosmic joke—the confusion between "self" and Self—is the most important "event" in all of spirituality. There are still great things to come, but ultimately if you go no further than discovering True Nature and experiencing relativity-ness as sort of a lucid dream, it's all good.

There are no further benefits for the unit, but I'm not saying this is the end of the rainbow.

302. When Awakeness first woke up through the Fred unit, Truth was so self-evident that the thought was, "Wow, this is so *simple*! Why doesn't *everybody* wake up?"

Fifteen years later I am astonished that *anyone* ever does. The dream is so very, *very* magnetic. Maya is so detailed and convincing. And "simple" is not kept in high regard by the oh-so-busy brains that want to figure all of this out.

Nowadays, whenever this teaching helps Awakeness notice Itself through a new unit, something in me is *bowled over* every single time it happens. There is no "getting used to" the full-blown miracle of Awakeness unveiling Itself *to* Itself!

This also seems to humble Fredness, but I notice said humility's duration is quite short!

303. A *misnamed* "awakening" is simply Awakeness

Itself, recognizing True Nature through the smokescreen of patterning and thus "breaking free" from the illusion of bondage. The false sense of being a separate, distinct entity drops, and Truth is all that remains.

No *personality* ever wakes up. There's nothing personal about it.

304. After you notice that everything is a dream, an emanation from Mind, notice that "*you*" are *also* in and of the dream. A dream character is writing this sentence, and a dream character is reading it. And then notice that it's not a dream, because that implies a beginning and an end. It's just *dreaming-ness*—the dreaming-ness that something exists and that something is in bondage.

305. To end seeking and proceed with clearing in post-awakening, we need to *accept* that "liberation" has occurred, that *This Is It*, and This Is It *As It Is right now*. There is no new territory we need to visit or wait for.

306. This whole "nondual thing" is about simplicity; it's about the obvious. But our big brains want to complicate it all. Our minds are trying to solve a problem that doesn't exist. Jesus said, "Truly I tell you, unless you change and become like little children, you will never enter the kingdom of heaven."

Jesus was a nondual teacher, and he knew what he was talking about. When you first came out of the womb, there was no sense of "me" or "other." There was no sense of duality at all, just unowned awe and wonder. You didn't know any more than I do now, which ain't much!

Child-Mind, with its innocence, awe, wonder, and majestic silence, is the tool you need to discover what's always already *right under your nose*.

307. Truth is always *right here*; it's just covered up by unskillful and untrue *concepts*. What we're *really* doing with these teachings is "encouraging Awakeness" to disidentify with the character you always thought you were—but aren't.

308. To use the Fred story as an example, let's understand that when a Fred-character is not *thought to be* in the room, there is clarity *already* present. Awakeness never revealed itself to a "Fred." The primary reason for that is that there *is no Fred.*

Clearing is not the process of clearing *up* the character. It is instead the process of clearing *out* the patterns of spontaneous, symbiotic conditioning that ego claims "work together" to form a make-believe character.

309. After awakening, whether it's minutes or months, unowned patterns we refer to as "ego" will almost inevitably arise and notice that it (ego) is still or again unsatisfied. The search for Self-as-other naturally resumes.

Notice that there are false references on both ends of that belief. There is no "other," and there is no centralized ego, only unowned patterns. There *is no* center.

310. If you thoroughly *grok* the innate unsatisfiability of unit-characters deep in your gut, you'll see the futility of trying to satisfy them. The momentum of seeking will automatically be reduced or eliminated.

You are *already* Oneness. You don't just "have it all"; you *are* it all. What can we "add" to *everything* to bring about an imaginary character's contentment?

311. Nondual inquiry is our most reliable defense against unconscious living. Inquiry is not passive; it is active. *Be willing* to remain alert (there are no instructions for this). Question thoughts as they arise. The key is not in what you *do*. It's what you are *willing* to do.

312. Doubts arise to Bobness and Susanness in post-awakening. Welcome to the norm. Notice first that they are *not* the Bob or Susan character's doubts. They can't be; there *is no* such character.

These doubts are spontaneous thought-patterns; they are conditioning rising to meet circumstance. They have no *owner*.

313. *You,* Awakeness, are not a thinker of thoughts. There *is no* thinker of thoughts. Thoughts appear and disappear, like fireworks in a dark sky.

Arising doubts *about* Truth cannot *be* Truth. They come and go; Truth does not. *You* do not. These thoughts cannot arise to or from an imaginary character. Understanding that they are not *Yours,* are You—whatever it is that You are—*required* to believe every thought that passes through?

314. I highly recommend pursuing any nondual inquiry using pen and paper. It's not *required,* but it helps us stay on point. Just this once, let's quit assuming we're the notable exception to all rules in life. Let's pretend, at least for now, that we're not the smartest person in every room we enter.

315. For me, rigorous inquiry was vital. I didn't formally pursue it every single day, but I did it *most* days—at least until it was well on its way to *undoing* "me."

It's okay to put off inquiry or to take it slow and easy. You don't even have to take it seriously. Feel free to suffer as long as you want.

316. Let me offer you a couple of suggestions on approaching nondual inquiry.

First and foremost, *notice the inquirer*. It may *feel like* a Bob or a Susan is the one asking questions, but given that there *is no* Bob or Susan, what are the odds that either one of these entirely *imaginary* characters are capable of initiating or following through with inquiry?

Impossible. So, who's left?

317. *Who or what is it* that is not to believe passing thoughts?

The default position for human beings is to believe thought. We cannot *not* believe thoughts until the "believer" is confirmed to be a hoax. This "seeing-through" is our real job here.

It is not something we *do*; it is something we *allow*.

318. Be *specific* with your inquiry. Go after one thought stream at a time until you have gone as far as you can go—*for now*. Pause, or leave inquiry altogether and return later.

For instance, just because you've discovered through inquiry that bank robbery can't *possibly* be your vocation any longer, don't expect to see through shoplifting or double-parking in that same moment. And never let "best" become the enemy of "better."

319. Catch yourself doing something *right*. When you notice that a question rises by itself to question thought, feel the *thrill* of that. Noticing a pattern after the fact still *counts*!

320. Nisargadatta Maharaj once asked a student, "Who told you that you are?" The student failed to answer, so Maharaj responded for him: "*Consciousness* tells you that you exist."

Yet consciousness itself comes and goes. Do you have a story in the *absence* of consciousness?

321. I always advise students and clients to "claim their awakening." What I mean is that until we're willing to recognize that we are *Awakeness Itself*—with no capacity for sleep—we will forever be chasing specific, delicious "states" where we either are, were, or will be "awake."

This is the Cosmic Joke, but if you're not in on it, it is not funny at all. Notice the false referencing. There's *no "personal you"* to achieve any other "state."

Incredibly, almost unbelievably, This—THIS VERY HAPPENING AS IT IS RIGHT NOW—is IT! And IT is YOU, Awakeness!

322. "Letting go of compulsive seeking" is another way to suggest allowing conviction to arise without interference. Just don't get in the way: there is nothing of interest for the character here.

323. Be alert and notice that you *are—right now.*
What notices this?
Only Knowingness can experience Knowingness.

Whence this experiencing?
There is No-thing before its appearance.
And No-thing upon its disappearance.
Does anything really happen?

Consciousness is an arising; it comes and goes.
It is not true.

It arises spontaneously upon the prospect of sentience and falls in tandem with its mortal host.
Does anything really happen?

324. Whenever there is a sense of cloudiness, find out whose it is. Then come back over and over again to the simple *sense* of existence, this *presently present* sense of aliveness.

Attention is the key to conscious living.

325. When delicious thoughts arise, and the craving to believe them is upon you, bend attention behind itself and rediscover what it was that woke up.

Then, stop.

326. Here are some examples of inquiry questions you might want to consider. Get to know them better than you know what you think is your own face. Later, formulate some on your own.

Try to be as open and alert as possible, and watch the questions automatically destroy your world. It's a beautiful thing.

Is the present debilitating thought *true?*

Is the thought that you think you just thought really an exception, or was it just *one more lying thought* attempting to sideline your attention? Call a spade a spade.

Where did this suffering-bringing thought come *from?*

Does that thought have an *owner?* Can you *find* one?

What is it like if, even for a few moments, you don't believe the automated thought-stream that arises from the mystery, is owned by no one, and goes nowhere?

Don't *think* about this; don't catalog it; *try* it! But try it *only* if you really want to wake up. Most seekers don't. How about you?

327. Remain alert and notice that you *are right now* what you have always been.
If there is an experience of oscillation, allow your attention to rediscover what it was that woke up.
Stop.

328. Awakening is a name for True Nature recognizing that it *is* True Nature.

You begin to see *from Yourself* instead of *as a unit*. You cut out the middleman.

329. We—Conscious Awakeness—always get lost in the *content* of the current arising. We don't really *see* it; we see *past* it. We are hungry for "next." We are hungry for "more."

When you recognize that you are *already* Oneness, the hunger for "next" and "more" begins to subside. As the belief in a character thins through nondual inquiry, we shift clockwise, like an elevator dial. We advance from a starting point of skepticism on through to hope, openness, and faith. Across the bridge of faith, there is a straight line to conviction.

Conviction bowls over anything in its path.

330. Nonduality is not about what's looked *at*. It's about *what's looking*.

331. When Awakeness grows tired of a given storyline, something subtle, yet dramatic, happens. The host unit becomes a *seeking* unit. We don't choose to walk the way of nonduality; the Way chooses us.

332. Be aware that through this teaching, we're forced into language. We may find languaging very helpful, but it is never *true*. We have to settle for it being skillful and *true-ish*.

333. This teaching does *NOT* encourage any attempt to avoid suffering with spirituality. The position here is to welcome each arising as it comes, regardless of its content. We will find no success in attempting to compare What Is to *what isn't*.

334. Ultimately, we can stand "only so much" suffering, an amount that varies dramatically from thought-character to thought-character. Most of us can endure such a large quantity of anxiety, worry, and fear that it never exceeds our capacity for suffering. For a few however, the *thought-character-in-the-head-that-we-think-we-are* completely *buckles* under the pressure.

The action of this buckling can play out in numerous ways. In extreme cases, it might show up as the imaginary character's so-called suicide, surrender, or insanity. Within relativity-ness, experiences are true, but relativity-ness itself is *not* true.

335. Where there is an inability to welcome This-As-It-Is, that apparent "failure" is fully accepted. Underneath that acceptance lies *willingness*, and a foundation of sincere willingness is all that is required.

There's no one home to foster willingness; it happens, or it doesn't. Regardless, cooperation with movement in the direction of acceptance appears to be helpful.

336. We are to take all reasonable and practical measures as new situations arise. Simultaneously, there is an experience of unshakable mental ease. Relativity-ness *counts*, but in the end, nothing within or about it really *matters*.

337. If we are pursuing the end of seeking, we have to STOP PURSUING IT to *find* it. We must "claim our awakening" to move beyond it. To proceed with clearing out the thought-character in post-awakening, we need to *embrace* the fact that we are and always have been Awakeness Itself.

We cannot *not* be IT, because there is nothing *other* than IT.

338. Once in a while a unit has declared that it has reached "spiritual freedom." That may be an *experience*, but if so, note that it is evidence of the *lack* of the thing it's presently declaring that it has. Freedom can only be experienced and remembered by an *imaginary* thought-character.

It is this phenomenon that we concern ourselves with here.

The sense of a "new freedom" shows up to replace an *experienced*, yet utterly *fictitious*, spiritual bondage. Outside of the thought-carnival of the mind, there *is no* spiritual bondage—never was and never could be.

If that seeking unit can let go of what it *thinks* it knows, what it *thinks* it is so cocksure of, then it becomes an empty and welcoming vessel, ready to be filled with Truth.

Personal knowledge seems like a lot to give up, even in exchange for personal wisdom. But the "letting-go crisis" will first diminish and finally disappear when it is finally realized there is *no one to give in,* and *nothing to give up.*

In actuality, Awakeness gives up *nothing* in exchange for *everything.* At that point, it can't be missed that everything is just fine—always has been and always will be.

339. By the time an arising is *noticed,* it's already over; it's in the can. One would do well to note that there is simply *no* future in resisting the past.

340. Sensing without introducing a story to accompany the sensing is neutral and impersonal. There *is no* one who senses. At that point, impersonal experiencing is *experiencing* the extraordinary impersonal experiencing that IT is.

Rest *in* and *as* this Knowledge.
The search is over; you are IT.
Let the character-idea go.

341. *This As It Is* is a perfect expression of That which is *prior* to This. Dare we tell ourselves the truth and acknowledge that *What Is* clearly and simply has the final say in *all* affairs. What Is lies beyond and above any sets of beliefs, opinions, or mental positions.

IT *Is.* Full stop.

342. Once awakening has occurred, see that there is no one here who could or should stake a claim to this apparent new (yet somehow familiar) territory. There is only This, and if we are bold enough to tell ourselves the truth, we can confess that we don't have so much as a *clue* as to what This is.

Nor do we know *what it is* that doesn't know what This is! This is a full circle that leads to the complete nullification of identity. Conditioning will continue to appear to be powered on, within relativity-ness. But we are not bound by it or to it. It is not "our personal conditioning."

343. Abidance is the ever-present Knowing of What You Are. It is not unit-knowledge. No one really knows IT; there is *only* IT.

344. Gradations of clarity and confusion naturally occur in post-awakening. To whom or what do they occur?

This is the only question that needs answering.

345. When the belief in a make-believe thought-character is not "invading" the Natural State, then by default there is clarity. Clearing is not the process of clearing an imaginary character *up*. It is the process of clearing reflexive conditioning and associative patterns of character-*ness* out.

There is no Fred, but there is plenty of Fredness. It's typing right now.

346. Awakening is when Awakeness recognizes Itself. Essentially your position moves from one of unconscious Awakeness to Conscious Awakeness. That's the "shift."

347. Waiting for enlightenment to arrive is like a bus at a bus stop, waiting for the bus to come.

348. Upon awakening, we finally "get" the cosmic joke. The dog has been chasing its tail! Consciousness has been looking *for* consciousness, when all the while IT has always already been looking *from* consciousness!

Take in that paragraph deeply. Read it, and let it hit You before You move on.

349. *Question*: How long do you think consciousness could look for consciousness without finding it?

Answer: Forever.

Explanation: When what you're looking *with* is what you're looking *for*, "finding" *cannot* happen.

350. We long for spiritual experiences. I know. I'm guilty; I did it, too. They're highly addictive. However, much to ego's disappointment, spirituality is not about what we're looking *at*, but rather *what it is* that's looking.

351. Enlightenment is not a process of addition; it is a process of subtraction. Every experience that happens while we're waiting for enlightenment to arrive is *already* the process of enlightenment playing itself out.

However, a make-believe thought-character will never see that. How could it?

It's just a make-believe thought-character!

352. Our problem is that we get hooked on clearing-to-prepare-for-enlightenment. And that *seems* to happen, but it's just a part of the dream. Oneness is seeking "something-else-over-there," which will soon be achieved by "someone-over-here."

For Oneness, however, let's notice there is no possibility for "something else," and there is no "over-there" over there. *This* is IT. The End.

353. We have continually sought distraction, because

consciousness, which spawns a sense of separation, is a heavy burden to bear. We have constantly and unsatisfactorily searched for something other than *This*. Something More-Bigger-Better.

That's a no-win pursuit. If we're not happy with what we already have, we're not going to be happy with whatever we get.

354. Abandoning the quest to *understand* What Is heralds the end of "becoming" and the conscious beginning of simply *being*.

355. When we realize deeply that these units are inherently unsatisfiable, we relax our grip. We then begin to sit with, in, and *as* This-As-It-Is, because Truth has been both noticed *and noted*.

No alternative.
No comparison.
Full stop.

356. Part of post-awakening is becoming comfortable with being *uncomfortable*.

Recognize, my dear Awakeness, that there can be tremendous and terrible injustice and discord in the world and that this has absolutely *nothing* to do with You. *You* are the Unborn, Unbound, and Untouched.

357. This virtual world is unimaginably complex with countless patterns, some working with each other and others in opposition. It is very much like a factory where there is serious disagreement on what the product is.

358. You are not *of* the world, nor are you genuinely *in* it. You are, quite simply, *beyond* it.

359. Stop seeking, and just notice what's already here, what has always been here, and what never changes. See deeply that, by definition, IT *cannot* be an object.

360. *What is it* that is trying to find "something else?" Can it be done?

361. When recognition of Truth occurs, we don't really come to *see* our True Nature. That's just convenient—and erroneous—languaging. Upon realization, we come to Know that what we thought of as the "personal me" is Awakeness in drag.

And then we see that this has always been the case. The pull for seeking is directly related to the level of belief one has in a separate seeker.

362. Awakening is the invitation to the dance; it's not the dance itself. Without *present* vigilance—which is more *attitude* than *action*—ego falls right back into the strange magnetism of the dream. The awakening is immediately claimed to have been a personal event by, about, and for the thought-character.

Conscious Awakeness immediately begins to fade out. "Our" experience of clarity quickly disappears, until it doesn't.

363. Abidance is the ever-present conscious Knowing of Who-we-are.

364. In the absence of the character, what can you find that is amiss? Nothing. To be present or to be mindful implies that there *is someone* to be mindful. The door to infinity is opened, not by being present, but by the willingness to be *absent.*

365. Clearing is the continual process of *thinning* the conditioning that automatically generates the sense of a thought-character, a false center to the mass of patterns surrounding it.

When we remain alert—meaning there is willingness to accept Truth *right now*—this spawns inquiry, thereby catching re-identification as it arises and piercing the veil of belief in the dream.

Essentially, we learn to allow the inevitable to take place as it was going to anyway, but without any judgment or interference.

366. Any apparent loss of clarity creates a panic for the thought-character. The Most Precious Thing "we" ever "had" has vanished! Now, "I"—the thought-character, the one who memory will falsely tell us "had got it" and "had it"—has now "lost it"!

This wholly imaginary "loss" is traumatic. We then drive ourselves and everyone around us crazy as we desperately try to figure out what we did wrong and what we can do to get "our personal awakening" back!

Ego's strategy is almost always to redouble "personal efforts" to "get it back." This efforting amounts to self-confirmation of the Big Two Lies we told ourselves to begin with.

The first lie is that there is a "personal me," and the second is that this "personal me" experienced a "personal awakening!"

You can have something personal, or you can have an awakening, but you can't have both simultaneously. One cancels out the other.

367. As you begin to pay conscious attention to attention, attention begins to pay conscious attention to you.

368. This is just a story, but it's close enough to truth to warrant sharing.

When Awakeness "gets tired of the localized story" and is pulled to come to know itself consciously, then the unit becomes a seeking unit. This seeking ultimately (but not necessarily permanently) ends up with Awakeness coming to know itself consciously.

However, much to everyone's surprise, the patterns and cycles of the thought-character persist. What changes is that we no longer *believe* this still-ongoing story.

369. Sensing, without introducing a story to accompany the sensing, is neutral and impersonal. The tremendous impersonal experiencing is *experiencing* the tremendous impersonal experiencing that IT is.

Sensing, *with* an accompanying personal story, is secondary dreaming within the primary dreaming. The primary dream, of course, is the dream of a "personal me".

This sensing and story-making each act to confirm the other, but both fail to refer to anything beyond imagination.

370. From the standpoint of character-life, spending a lot of time in the company of sages is perhaps the most important thing you can do to wake up or foster clarity in post-awakening.

But let us not undersell the power of simply paying attention to attention. Note that the *frequency* of doing so is more important than the *duration*.

371. In post-awakening there is often an initial sense of sadness or grief for the loss of our favorite illusion, meaning the loss of the sense of a separate identity that has free agency.

But typically, there also arises a new, background Knowing that all is well. This "Great Unknowing" comes with the Seeing that the experienced universe is the only way it could possibly be. Krishnamurti said that "all suffering begins with comparison," and he was right!

372. Without referring to memory, tell me what you are. Yes, I discovered the same thing that you just did: *we don't know.*

Don't fret. It is *far* better to know that you *don't* know what you are than it is to *think* you know when you don't. Whatever you are cannot be conceptualized. If you think you know, it's a sure sign that you're both oblivious and confused.

373. *This* teaching is about how to be mindless—and not care. This is an *unteaching* about what you think you know.

374. Increased clarity arrives when there is progressively less and less identification with the thought-character. What feels like "growing clarity" is really just the thinning of our attachment to the character. We are not here to clear Bob up. There is no Bob. We are here to clear Bob*ness out.*

375. In early awakening, typically, the sense of being a witness is quite profound. Just as one of my teachers told me, I have found that "the witness" is just another thought, an experience. It is an initial protective mechanism that provides a sense of distance from relativity-ness. In other words, it's the experience of a still-extant, if very subtle, thought-character.

As clarity progresses, it's seen that there is no

separation of any kind anywhere, so there can be neither witness nor witnessed. There is only *witnessing*. Wholeness cannot be objectively observed. There is no subject-object. There is an *experience* of subject-object, which weakens in post-awakening but does not disappear completely. It is simply seen through more quickly and easily, and we cease to take it seriously.

376. The enhanced perception we so often experience in post awakening is not due to some thought-character seeing more and more subtly. It's Awakeness experiencing Itself through less and less thought-character. Our conviction in relativity-ness morphs into conviction in Truth.

377. I might declare that we are addicted to the sense of separation, provided there was a "we" here. There is not.

There is only Wholeness, which has no parts, no seams, no division of any kind *whatsoever*.

Wholeness merely *dreams* of Partness and then starts

believing in a "me" *part*, which is made possible only through the mirror belief in an "other" *part*. But really, there is no "me," no "other." No "other," no "me."

Wholeness first dreams of duality, then comes to believe in what was dreamed, and subsequently declares the *dream* to be *reality*. During all of this unconscious shuffling, the question "What is it that is dreaming?" is completely forgotten or ignored.

378. The process of clearing is not one of "Fred" progressing into deeper Awakeness. It is Awakeness experiencing ever more frequent Fred-free moments. Whenever there is a character-free moment, you have removed what is false, leaving what is true to shine by itself.

379. When I wake up in the morning, habit immediately slips my glasses onto my face. Before that, Awakeness, in a similar way, has already "slipped into this unit," so to speak.

380. The *first* (and automatic) believed thought for everyone everywhere, *every single time*, is, "I am a Susan," or "I'm a Bob." Consciousness' core identification with an imaginary unit *is* the unseen entrance to the rabbit hole!

We believed this was "Susan's dream," when in fact it is Susan that is the dream!

Once that first thought is believed, the second automatic thought immediately arises. This second thought is, "There is a problem here (for me)," or perhaps the slight variation that declares, "Things should be other than the way they are." Often, there is a third automatic and believed thought, "And *I* need to fix it."

Not only do these thoughts assume an independent "I", but they also assert an imperfect reality, both of which are categorically incorrect and absurdly ridiculous.

Every believed thought is confirmation of a completely imaginary thought-character. The start of the story is based on a false reference: "I am Bob." There is Bob*ness*, but there is no Bob. Hurricane Bob is wet and windy, but there's no "Bob" in the center of it.

I think you'll have great difficulty discovering what it is that's stating, "I am," as well.

The Great Argument is begun with the first step taken

in misidentification. Only awakening can break that hypnosis.

381. So long as there is complaining, the focus of attention is on the *complaint*, and there is no investigation into the "complainer." Shift your attention: *What is it* that is so unhappy and discontent?

382. You are like an infinite beach that sometimes dreams it is only a single grain of sand. Does that dreaming actually *transmute* an endless beach into a single grain of sand? Of course not. Does *dreaming* that one is rich or poor change the dreamer's financial position?

383. We hear about people *experiencing* emptiness. This statement is a languaging error.

When someone reports that they have "experienced"

emptiness, there is always some residual character identification claiming that *someone* experienced *no-thing*! By the very "name and nature" of *no-thing*, this is patently impossible.

What *is* true is that following some *verbally unrelatable incident*, the *sense* that someone experienced no-thing can arise. We just need to see that this particular thought, like *all of our thoughts*, is *not* true.

384. We have night-dreams where there are no rules, and that's easily accepted. Following our night-dreams we have day-dreams where there are also no rules. Anything can happen anywhere at any time, but we don't want to hear about it.

385. This is always already *only* the Oneness experience that's being experienced *by* Oneness. Those who say, "I understand this intellectually, but it is not my experience," have it exactly *backward*.

Oneness is *always* your experience, and if you think that you are *not* having the "Oneness experience," it is because you feel that you are something *other than* Oneness. Is that even *possible*?

386. True abidance is knowing yourself to be the divine at all times, even when the unit is not acting in what we presume to be an "enlightened" fashion. Units do what they do. There's nothing other than conditioning and circumstances *dictating* the behavior; it just *happens*. Life happens. Or at least it appears to.

If we notice an unskillful pattern, then what is *seeing* that unskillful pattern is not *part* of that pattern. The only thing that can spot unconsciousness is alert consciousness.

387. Once you think that you are an individual, the second believed thought automatically arises: "*What Is* should be *other* than it is." It doesn't matter what the current arising looks like. These units are inherently unsatisfiable. Neither the body nor the thought-character wake up. They don't have the capacity for that.

It is *Awakeness* that has the so-called "awakening." Awakeness moves from a state of unconsciousness into consciousness. Unconscious Awakeness thinks it knows pretty much everything. Conscious Awakeness knows Itself and nothing else.

388. After years of extensive investigation, I have to confide that—amazingly—there is no "Fred" to be found. There is only *This*. This is IT. There's no more or less of IT, no coming and going of IT, no inside or outside of IT, and there's no way to get around or out of IT.

There is *only* This-Here-Now.

389. In the absence of a Fred-character, This-Here-Now seems to be quite enough. The ideas of "more" or "other" are merely mad thoughts arising from insanity. If those thoughts are taken seriously, we suffer. If they aren't, we don't. What part of that is so hard to understand?

390. In order for me to host a "successful" Awakening Session, I need a client who is willing and able to recognize the truth when it is presented to them. Rather sadly, this apparent decision is not the client's call.

All that can ever "wake up" is Awakeness Itself. If Awakeness "is ready" to notice what is already *startlingly obvious*, then it will. It can't *not*.

However, if Awakeness is still finding ample distraction in experiencing the drama of suffering, it won't. It *can't*.

I think this teaching is primarily focused on the border between these unknown territories of "ready" and "not-ready." This teaching is a means by which Conscious Awakeness recognizes unconscious Awakeness for what *it isn't*, after which the total misunderstanding of the statements, "I'm awake," or "I'm *not* awake," drops away. It happens, or it doesn't; there is no right or wrong to it. The inevitable unfolds as it must.

There is no "teaching" per se.

391. It takes great honesty to wake up the first time, and that's also what it takes to "come back to clarity" every time after that. Of course, it's not a thought-character's honesty. Imaginary beings cannot *be* or *do* anything—they're *imaginary*. Awakeness has to give up on playing the riveting game it has been playing with itself.

In the end, it will do so, or it won't. However, when Conscious Awakeness actively and knowingly begins to work with its unconscious Self, incredible things can and do unfold. Nonetheless, the whole idea of one *unit* (the enlightened wonder) trying to wake up another *unit* (the slow, rather dense one) is total nonsense.

Regardless, that false teaching and training are the central focus of the spiritual scene, nondual or otherwise. It has always been this way, and I see no end in sight.

392. Awakeness is always here and always clear, and there is nothing outside of it. Given this truth, *what can it be* that seems to move in and out of clarity?

393. Enlightenment is all about *right now*. The term "character" is what we use to describe Awakeness when it is under the influence of believed thought. The first big dive *out* of clarity is when the first thought is owned and believed. The first believed thought is, "I am a Susan or a Bob," or what have you.

394. Identification with the body always seems to be a

sticking point. There is no graduation to permanent state of no-self. We are always clearing Fred out: Awakeness noticing the absence of Fred.

395. Nothing is to be found "outside" or "other than" Awakeness because there is no "outside" or "other than" Awakeness. You are That which does not move.

396. Keep in mind that oscillation—the sense of losing or gaining clarity—is a high-quality problem. You've had a glimpse or perhaps multiple glimpses of True Nature; you may have even had interludes of abidance *as* Truth. How many yearn and continue to search for just a taste of that?

397. We keep thinking that we are going to reach a point of having a *permanent* sense of abidance. Yet it's just a false reference to some vague "center" that simply doesn't exist. There is no center to "achieve stasis within enlightenment." As ever, language leads us astray.

My own experience indicates that there is a *sense* (only) of some unfindable "I" that is consciously cognizant of this arising. There is a *present* recognition that only Awakeness Itself can be said to exist. And more truthfully, Awakeness is beyond existing or not existing.

Yesterday's insight is like yesterday's newspaper.

398. As the *sense* of our being an *impossibly* "separate and central character" begins to thin out, so does the belief that there was ever anything at all in the midst of those patterns. When a tornado wears out, there remains nothing but a memory of transformed air.

399. If we come to nonduality in search of gain, we will be deeply disappointed. We have to come here in search of *loss.* We must *lose* the false ideas that we came with! Clearing is not replacing old patterns of thought with newer, better patterns of thought. Clearing is the dropping away of hypnotic patterns that occur naturally upon our noticing This as self-evident truth.

400. Awakening is the initial, often instantaneous, recognition of who you are not and then (perhaps) of who you really are. Clearing is the experientially gradual dissolution of believed character patterns. There is the rising conviction that there are no true thoughts and that who you really are is prior to and beyond language.

Conviction arises, but there is no owner to it. Your disguise as a unit becomes less convincing, and the dream of duality becomes less enchanting—and thus less "sticky."

401. There is no satisfying the person who believes that This is too little. The story of a *coming* satisfaction is the dream itself in action.

402. Remember that it's only the thought-character that seems to *oscillate* between the absolute and relativity-ness. Awakeness never oscillates. You cannot rest *in* awareness. You can only rest *as* awareness.

403. If you notice you're "asleep," you're not actually asleep, because That which is noticing is Awakeness itself.

404. We almost exclusively pay attention to apparent objects, instead of the space that holds them. But the space is more essential. It is always there; it does not come and go. We are addicted to *distraction*—to change, the sense of separation, and thought.

Consciousness is a burden, and we will do almost anything to avoid noticing it.

405. The first believed thought for every human everywhere all the time is, "I'm a Bob," or "I'm a Susan."

The second believed thought then kicks in automatically. No one does it; it just happens, and it's always in the form of a complaint. "I'm not as clear as I should be," or "I'm 'separated' from Oneness," or "I'm an individual," or "I'm right," or "Something is wrong here."

406. You are the very same Awakeness that shone through the great sages. When we declare, "I'm not awake," that is simply Awakeness unwittingly commenting on a given unit's conditioning and belief system. It's never true.

407. Clarity is "being lived" without any backtalk.

408. It's not *answers* that free us; it's *questions*.

409. We have to *not* know right *now*. That's all we need to know.

410. The purpose of inquiry is to instill doubt, which clears out sureness. Sureness is the death of spiritual progress. Doubt is our friend here. It is what we want to entertain.

411. Become comfortable with uncertainty, until it is no longer uncomfortable.
Be patient with the unit and learn to love the process.

412. We operate on assumptions. There can be no clarity until we begin to question our most basic beliefs. Whatever comes into your head, persistently ask, "Is that true?" or "Who is the author of that thought?" or simply, "Who wants to know?"

There is no strategy. Just ask and pause to hear the answer. No meaningful answer will arise, but the mind will stop and the question will fade.

413. We must back away from *relative* truth to see the greater truth.

"Neti, Neti. I am not *limited* to this body, this mind, these thoughts; I am not *limited* to the universes of worlds and dimensions, nor their content."

We need to see what isn't true if we are ever to see What Is. Meet the world with inquiry.

414. Practice is an expression of the willingness to be an empty teacup. Then you can be filled from the bottom to the rim.

415. What this teaching does is to change the default point of view from which the world is met. The default position was previously: as the character-unit. Now, it is: *as* the Absolute. Where we are looking *from* dictates what we are looking *at*.

416. What's untrue cannot stand against the power of inquiry.

417. Can you find an *owner* of this awareness? We already know you can make one up. The question is, can you *locate* one?

418. *What is* it that is engaging in inquiry? Can you *locate* an inquirer?

419. We need to ask ourselves the same questions or hear the same pointers again and again. *Repetition is the mother of clarity*, and enlightenment is all about *right now*.

420. It is vital to notice who the *viewer* of "our viewpoint" is. Is this arising being viewed from the "eyes of Awakeness" or from the eyes of a so-called "personal me?"

Awakeness will experience the perfect expression of Itself, which we term What Is.
The view of a "personal me" will deliver endless empty opinions *about* What Is.

We don't suffer from What Is. We suffer from our own commentary on What Is.

421. When our default view shifts from belief and narrow-mindedness over to inquiry and openness, we abide *as* the Now. Our experiencing is without comparison or alternative. *This* is freedom from imagination, which seemingly held us in bondage.

422. After immersion in the process of nondual inquiry, a point will be reached where inquiry essentially does itself. But that point cannot occur in the absence of alertness. Paying *conscious* attention *to* attention is key. The pattern of automated belief slowly morphs into the passive practice of inquiry.

423. When unchallenged thoughts arise, they transmute into beliefs. They don't arise from anywhere, nor do they arise to anyone. Nonetheless, they arise, and they fall.

Beliefs are impermanent patterns of thought. Yet, they typically will not be seen through unless we question them. Most seekers have some gradation of raw wakefulness, and some have a lot. This is *not* the same thing as clarity. We must be alert enough to challenge beliefs, and from that questioning, clarity arises.

424. Complacency is the death of spiritual progress. There is a *massive* difference between complacency and Conviction. Saying to yourself or others "I got it!" is a lie. That is just self-satisfaction in an incomplete effort.

Peaceful abidance *as* both nothing and everything is Conviction.

425. Faith is the weaker sibling of Conviction, but it takes faith to *discover* Conviction. Upon that discovery, faith vanishes; there is no further need of it.

426. The spiritual journey is like an elevator dial. It starts with skepticism, moves through suspicion, to doubt, until even that doubt disappears. Ramana Maharshi told us, "Doubt is the last thing to go." He was right, because the absence of doubt *is* Conviction.

427. Who are you in the absence of memory?
Check.

428. Conviction is what is left when there is no longer

any question of who or what you are. The localized experience here is that the process took a lot of "time." However, Conviction is outside of time or state. We don't *reach* it; we *are* IT.

429. Is there a past *right now?*
Is there a future *right now?*
Is there anything *other than* right now?
There are lots of *stories*, but where are the *facts?*

430. When equanimity is disturbed, ask yourself, "What thought was just believed? Where or who is the *owner* of this thought?" When penetrated, thoughts dissipate. However, initially, only the most obvious untruths dissipate, but more subtle untruths may linger.

This is like a freshly awakened bank robber who suddenly sees that robbing banks is *wrong*. So far, so good. He prays to God in gratitude that he can still earn his living by shoplifting!

431. Are the thoughts that occur *your* thoughts? Are you intentionally thinking these thoughts? Are you generating these thoughts?

432. To what or whom are these thoughts occurring *to*? Not a character, that's for sure, because there *is no* character. That's just a story about an invisible friend.

Thoughts simply *happen*. You can't *stop* a train of ideas because you're not *causing* them. They just arise on their own, *from* no one, *to* no one.

433. Bring alertness to "unskillful" patterns (e.g., eating too much, watching too much TV), and let go of the guilt, shame, and blame, which only serve to reinforce those patterns. I have come to have very low expectations of this unit. It does what it does. If I can't accept this body/mind, then I certainly won't be able to accept the world.

434. In all interactions, know that when you're speaking, you are never talking to anyone other than YourSelf. Every day I help MySelf/YourSelf wake up through different lenses all over the world.

435. Hot asphalt plus a sprinkling rain will cause steam to rise from the pavement. Who is doing that? No one, of course. The conditions simply *are*; nobody is *doing* them. Relative action is merely conditioning rising to meet circumstance. You could simply *witness* thoughts. It is only through habit that Awakeness, via the dream character, takes delivery of them.

UPS comes to my door nearly every day. If the UPS man rings, it means I have to sign for something. If he has brought a box that I don't want to accept, I don't have to take delivery of it. He won't push past me to leave it on our coffee table; he just carts it away.

I don't have to take delivery of everything that arrives at my front door. Do *you*?

436. I've come to have very meager expectations of this unit. I notice that it does what it does. If we can't accept the inevitable unfolding of experience through a single given unit, then how will we ever come to terms with the unavoidable metamorphosis of the world?

The experienced human world of opposites and the appearance of change *is* the world of relativity.

437. When you wake up, you gradually come to see the unit's unskillful patterns. Don't take ownership of them; they're not yours.

What is *noticing* the patterns is outside of the patterns, and *that* is what you really are. Awakeness notices the unskillfulness; the unit may react with distress and shame. But look and see that you are not only the character. You are everything, while at the same time you are nothing.

A key mantra is, "Everything *counts*, but nothing *matters*. Nonetheless, everything still counts!"

Where is the personal shame in a universe where what happens *could not have not happened*? Within relativity-ness, however, the body is still going to take the rap. Within the *scope of the dream*, that which we think of as "karma" has a very long arm indeed. There is *overall* balance in relativity. There has to be. That's just the way IT works.

438. Most of us had a vision of what we'd be like after awakening. We would be mindful, serene, compassionate, and loving. Bad habits, uncouth or unconscious behavior, would cease. Or so we wished. Why not accept what you find until you find something else?

Soon enough we discover that, for the most part, the mind-body unit continues to play out its same old patterns. They get buffed and polished, but some of them will be persistent. There may be changes in the personality, even wonderful and transformative growth. Nonetheless, sagacity is not necessarily saintly.

Awakeness must surrender to the character—*as it is*, here and now. It makes sense to cooperate with the inevitable, but let's notice that there is no *character* which could ever surrender to God. That's another pointer, pointing in the wrong direction.

Through it all, you are always bright, always perfect. Weather changes; the sky does not. Just be willing to remain alert, whether you do or you don't. Your only job is to shine.

439. Bring *conscious* consciousness to "unskillful" patterns and allow it to shine upon your sense of guilt, shame, and blame. These feelings serve only to reinforce unskillful patterns. How to let go? Don't *try*. Simply allow the natural light of attention to dissolve the darkness—*at its own pace.*

440. Relativity-ness, by its very existence, is resistance to unconditioned space. Yet this same space never resists relativity-ness. Let the mind-body unit be as it is. The only thing wrong is that the unit *thinks* there is something wrong with the unit's experience—*for which there is no comparison or alternative.*

441. When we change from telling stories to telling the truth, we recognize Who we are; we start to live as we really are and come to willingly accept life on life's own terms.

442. Notice when ego "comes back in," when it arises. This is not a problem. It's a pattern and will run until it's seen that the pattern is no longer warranted. These patterns, the conditioning of so-called "individual" units interacting within a seemingly separate world, mask the truth. Although there is no Fred to thin out, as Fred*ness* thins, the truth becomes *more* obvious, with increasing frequency and duration. There may still be the scent and sense of "I," but see that they have no owner.

443. The unit will always have preferences, and as long as you identify YourSelf as the unit, you will always have preferences. If you don't identify with the unit, preferences will become quite secondary and optional!

All preferences are illusion. The absolute has no preferences about the unit's preferences. It has unconditional acceptance of you. The character will continue to appear to have preferences, but you will come to hold them lightly. You can't discover anything new so long as you are clinging to the old.

444. The more time we spend outside the dream, the less tolerance we have for being in it. Awakeness beholds the creativity and diversity of relativity-ness with delight and curiosity. However, upon subscribing to the myth of separation, we suffer, because we are living in direct contradiction to Truth.

445. Relativity-ness is the interplay between attraction and aversion. Notice it and drop it. Don't even name it. No commentary. No scolding. When you see that movement, just notice it. Any commentary is coming from the character, and what notices the commentary has no comment.

446. Occasionally we will catch ourselves in what we deem an unskillful action or thought. What catches this? OurSelf—Conscious Awakeness. The less unit identification, the clearer the view.

Awakeness is always here. Watch conditioning as it

arises. Notice it without judgment or projection. Deconditioning will occur naturally.

447. What "sees" nonjudgmentally is Awakeness, but what responds to circumstances is conditioning. If you notice an unskillful pattern, don't be shocked or appalled.

Remember that what woke up is Awakeness, not some apparently personal dream-conditioning. There is a victory in being alert to *this* moment. When we note a pattern, attention is what notices it. Patterns are within relativity-ness, but That which sees the patterns is not.

448. Awakeness Itself is always the Inquirer. Inquiry does not occur in the absence of alertness. Patterns of automated belief are exchanged for the more alert pattern of inquiry. When done with earnestness, the alert pattern of inquiry becomes automated. Change proceeds gradually as we observe without judgment.

There is *no judge*.

449. When these units become vehicles for awakening, they stand with one foot in the absolute and one in relativity. Welcome to post-awakening.

450. We eventually reach the stage where we begin to notice unskillful patterns by their absence.

451. As Oneness, what part of me do I fear? What part of me do I hate?

452. Awakeness is as present as it can be through every unit in every circumstance. Conditioning plus conditions determine all relative outcomes. This is neither failing nor succeeding. Here/Now simply is as it is Here/Now.

When we try to get *to* Awakeness, we create an imaginary character who's estranged from Here/Now. It's lunacy. We identify with that character and impose ideas about how Here/Now should be, look, or feel.

And we wonder why there is so much suffering!

453. You are That: inexpressible, unimaginable, un-language-able, inexperienceable.

454. The mind tries to *hold* the "experience" of awakening. It can't. The part cannot contain the whole of which it is a part. However, we can use the mind to *behold* Awakeness.

455. Even the "witness" is just another thought, another concept. There is no witnesser, and there is no witnessed. There is just witness*ing* happen*ing*.

456. Just because you experience something does not mean that the experienced is true. The experience is *valid*, but we can't reify it. All concepts, all thoughts, are false. The sky *looks* blue, but when you put it in a bottle, *is it* blue?

457. Pan over the room with your cellphone. What is your camera thinking about the content? Nothing. How many *things* is the camera "seeing?"

The lens finds just *one* thing; it cannot differentiate. It merely reflects relativity-ness; it cannot, does not, think. But when mind is brought to the camera, conceptualization and differentiation *explode*.

The camera, however, just reflects light. The camera is "standing as awareness." You can mimic this and find Truth Here/Now.

458. In the absence of language, what do you find?

459. Look through the mind-body unit without engaging in the thoughts of the unit. What is looking has no center or boundaries. When the body is being consciously used as a sensing device, there is only Oneness to be seen. It is *thought* that carves out categories. The Tao that can be named is *not* the eternal Tao.

460. Whatever You are, IT is prior to language. We can come to know "Who" we are, in the sense that we would be able to speak plainly with Jesus or Buddha, but we cannot tell you *what* that "Who-*ing*" is. We don't know!

Do we *care*? We cannot hope to *explain* That which is beyond either explanation or description. We cannot *think* about That which is *prior* to thought. Nor can we experience That which is outside of the field of experience.

There is Knowing, but there is no one to claim it.

461. You are the raw *potentiality* for consciousness. In the absence of consciousness, however, you are not aware. You are beyond the reach of opposites, beyond "are" or "are not."

Note that a lack of experience is not in itself an experience.

462. Consciousness is the saloon door that swings into and out of the paradox of Void/duality. "I am," which is the *first story,* the first experiencing, is at the farthest edge of duality. It is the finger pointing at the moon, but it is not the moon.

463. There are no true thoughts. Some are "true-*ish*" or "truth-*like*," and some are closer to truth than others, but *none* of them are *true.*

464. "No-thing" is pure potentiality and thus imperceivable. IT is beyond "is" or "is not", beyond "alive" or "dead"—simply *Beyond.*

465. There are no true statements in this teaching. "I" aim for precision in "my" teaching, said the Cheshire Cat to the White Rabbit, but anything I say is at best only a provisional truth. Provisional truths, while not wholly accurate, can nonetheless prove to be very helpful within the dream.

466. Silence is the most accurate teaching, but it is not the most efficient. Plus, by going around our elbow to get to our thumb, there is a sublime pleasure in our attempts to express the inexpressible.

467. The human brain is like the grain of sand in a cement truck that's pretty sure it knows what's going on. The finite cannot comprehend the infinite.

468. Part of clearing up is learning how to hear and use ordinary language without believing it, so you can fully experience this dream without believing in the absolute reality of it.

469. When we recognize that a thought is being believed, we use inquiry to try and find the owner of it. There is no owner of thoughts. They arise because of interior and exterior conditioning. We cannot stop thoughts, but we can allow them to pass, without believing them. The moment the thought is snatched up and owned, it takes on a sense of importance and truth. The first thought is identification with Fred. The second thought is that something is wrong here.

470. The unit cannot "drop the witness." Only Awakeness can notice there *is no* witness.

471. Which is closer to the truth of your experience, the *thought* "I am" or the *felt* "sense of being?" Does a *sense* of something necessarily represent the *truth* of anything?

472. Consciousness can come to recognize its own consciousness, but that which is *prior* to consciousness cannot *be known* by consciousness. In this same way, that which *precedes* thought or experience cannot be either thought *about* or experienced.

We cannot *know* IT, but we can *be* IT. In fact, we *cannot not* be IT, given that there is only one thing going on. And we can *actively* know *of* IT, a Knowing which is the sweetest nectar of the gods.

473. Relativity-ness is, by necessity, all about *contrast.* For the absolute, there is *no* contrast, hence no experience.

474. I am not that which the Tao is acting either upon or through; *I am the Tao.*

475. You don't—*can't*—know yourSelf in the absence of consciousness. The sense of being, of "aliveness," is consciousness devoid of identification, subject to the relative presence of a body. "I am" is when belief arises that the amorphous "sense of being" is the "center" of a boundless field of experience.

But of course, no boundaries also means no center.

476. "Am I the vastness, or am I a human?" The brain wants to know. You are not either-or; you're *both.* You are not limited to being a single object. You are the underlying fountain of *all* things.

477. There is no birth, death, or reincarnation. The Animating Presence that is *currently experiencing "you"* cannot "return" because it can't leave Itself to begin with! Whatever This is, IT is *all* there is. There's no inside or outside to IT, no before or after.

478. Close your eyes and relax. Notice the sense of presence within the dark field. The sense of being is not localized. There is just a sense of presence, of "hereness." No me. A vastness. No boundaries. No qualities. A sense of undulation or underlying energetic movement. You are prior to existence and experiencing. There is no experience of birth or death for Awakeness. You are the unborn, unbound, and untouched.

479. Beings, objects, circumstances, events are arisings within the undifferentiated soup. And the undifferentiated soup is an overlay to the nothingness beneath it. There is *one* thing going on within the dream of relativity-ness. The Absolute is *No*-thing.

It is a world of empty experiencing. Everything exists only relative to everything else. No-thing is neither happening nor not happening.

480. There is a *pattern* of being. There is a *sense* of being. But *apparent* "beingness" is not the *ground* of being. No-thing is the stage upon which *appearances* of beingness come and go. Beingness springs from the ground of being—That which can neither be experienced nor described.

481. True Nature is space-like. Notice that the only thing that doesn't come and go is space itself. All appearances arise and fall within IT.

Space is the great *uniter*, not the great *divider*.

482. The mind wants to know, "If there is only

Oneness, and I am IT, why can't I experience swimming upstream as a salmon?"

You *are* experiencing it—*as* the salmon.

483. What's looking through those eyes is the same thing that's looking through these. And through every sentient being—simultaneously.

484. All manifestation arises from consciousness, which itself is the first arising, and it comes and goes. Consciousness spontaneously arises from the absolute, the void, the unfathomable. It vanishes in the same way.

485. The sense of being is the first deception. You are prior to that. You know beingness, but beingness can't know you.

486. There is only dream*ing*—no dreamer, no dreamed.

487. I am the Source of all dreaming. Nothing can happen without me.

488. I know "who" I am, but I haven't a clue as to *what* That is.

489. The ultimate understanding is coming to the understanding that there *is no* understanding This.

490. If there is a desire for either peace or clarity, attempting to understand what is not understandable must be abandoned.

491. You are neither awake nor not-awake. You are Awakeness itself.

492. Experiencing or the ceasing of experiencing has no effect on you whatsoever.

493. We experience the world of the born, but That which experiences This is the Unborn.

494. The void is emptiness, yet that No-thing is full to the brim and rich beyond imagination. That is the *potential* for This.

495. Arisings appear upon the featureless ground of being. They look distinct but are not separate from the ground of being. "We" experience "them," even though "we" are to be counted among the arisings. Suffering occurs when we take ownership of these appearances. Once they cease, the ground of being remains, untouched.

496. Ego wants information about a death it will never experience. There is no opposite to life; there is only *Life-ing*. Content changes, but That *within which* the content changes does not change. You are Unborn and thus cannot die.

497. A spiritual experience is sometimes a sidecar to truth. The experience is secondary; the payload is primary. A perfect experience is the one that helps us see Truth so clearly that it cannot be unseen and is then allowed to vanish without regret.

498. Someone's desire to *regain* an awakening experience is the ego's desire to "relive" an experience it never had to begin with. We keep expecting Conscious Awakeness to show up *for* the character, but Conscious Awakeness only shows up in the absence *of* the character.

499. Addiction to spiritual experience is the death of spiritual growth. There is only one thing going on. It has to be *this*, and it has to be *now*.

500. One of the biggest post-awakening shifts I had occurred one evening when I was having a love affair with a TV cabinet. (This is another example of Oneness pretending to be twoness.)

There was a deep, intimate sense of love and unity. I felt a sense of sadness when I grew sleepy, knowing that this state would be gone when I awoke the next morning. Out of nowhere a voice popped up that said, "Don't worry; it'll be back."

The following morning the unity experience had passed, but the sense of frustration that accompanied the loss was not present. I was Awakeness whether I knew it, or felt like it, or not! THIS was a new freedom!

There have been lots of "keen moments" since that night, but there has been no more clinging to them.

501. The surest way to know that you are in an altered state is if there is a craving *for* an altered state! Awakeness is not an altered state; it is our natural state. Abidance *as This* clears the desire for bigger, better, more, and other.

502. Another big shift occurred the day I ceased demanding that relativity show up in a specific, character-centered way. I spent half a century trying to cover the world with leather when all I ever needed to do was put on a pair of shoes.

I quit requiring conditions to match my wishes and instead began to modify my view. At that point, there is no desire beyond the present conditions.

503. You can't get "disconnected" from what you *are.*

504. A so-called spiritual experience is the experience of Awakeness "waking up," translated through a character view. In truth you are always having a spiritual experience, because there is *only* spiritual experience.

505. In this present moment, if you are pretending to "not be awake," then Oneness is telling Oneness that Oneness is not having the Oneness experience.

My question is, "What other experience can you have?"

506. You can't get closer to truth than *where* you are.

507. Fred Davis expected to experience "the Truth of God" one day. What actually happened was that Truth discovered the fiction of a "Fred Davis."

508. There is a sense of someone making "spiritual progress," and that is a reasonably skillful term, but there is no *actual* spiritual progress. The hamster may stand up and flex its new muscles, but then it gets back on its wheel.

509. The fundamental error is the belief that Fred will have a deep spiritual insight. But there is no Fred to experience insight. Awakeness shows itself only in *conscious Fred-free* moments.

510. Typically, we first awaken to what we are *not*. We are not the body, mind, thoughts; we are nothing in or of this world. If we are lucky, during what will be experienced as "sometime later," we awaken to what we really are. Most initial awakenings are "incomplete"— so to speak.

511. True nonduality recognizes that Awakeness *includes* the world of relativity.

512. Students regularly ask, "How do I *not* live as a character when the *experience* of a "separate me" is still ongoing?"

Confusion arises when you have seen that you are nothing, but you have not yet seen that you are everything. Nihilism can and often does occur if we ignorantly refuse to move beyond this point.

Yet there's no cause for dismay. There's no "you" there to get "your" awakening wrong. Everything happens as it must, which includes "your personal awakening" experience.

513. When we recognize that we are not *just* nothing, we come to see that we are also *everything*.

514. "You" are unborn, unbound, and untouched.

When the sense of control and cause and effect drop,

allow judgment to drop as well. Judgment never arises from the Absolute; it is always from the character-view, and it is always about the character's world. It has nothing to do with You.

515. Real embodiment is when the body becomes a friction-free vehicle for the Tao. Everything is exactly as it has to be—although content can change instantaneously.

516. Ultimate freedom is the result of Awakeness accepting relativity-ness.

517. Conventional awakening is awakening to what you're *not*. It is clearly seen that there is "no one at home" within the body. Yet, it is impossible to "live as a negative."

Ultimately, if we are going to live (more correctly, if we are going to *be lived*) stably and clearly, we have to see and accept not only what we are *not*, but also what we *are*. As Nisargadatta Maharaj states, "Love says: 'I am everything.' Wisdom says: 'I am nothing.' Between the two my life flows."

Abandoning either view is an invitation to suffering.

518. I cannot ditch vastness in favor of Fredness, and I cannot ditch Fredness in favor of the vastness. They are two simultaneous aspects of the same thing, and they both have to be honored. That's the full embrace: wholeness *and* part-ness.

519. The magnetic force of the dream is so strong that minutes after awakening people will sometimes ask, "So, how do I live?" I always suggest that you be alert to which way the wind is blowing and be willing to move in that direction.

520. The experience of separation is not a mistake—there are no mistakes. The sense of separation is the only way by which You can know and experience Yourself objectively.

521. Illusions are not a problem unless we believe them. Our single problem is believing that we are human beings who have a problem. Neither belief is true.

522. What can be seen from the Absolute view may be Absolutely true, but that doesn't make it *relatively* true. And what is seen from the relative viewpoint may be relatively true, but that doesn't make it *Absolutely* true.

If we are grabbing or rejecting one side or the other, we have Absolutism or Relativism but not nonduality. Nonduality is never this *or* that. Nonduality is always This *and* That.

This truth is an impossible paradox for the brain to wrap itself around, which is why we ultimately have to abandon the *search* for truth to *recognize* Truth.

523. When operating within relativity-ness, so long as it *feels as if* there is someone in the body to make a decision, make the wisest, most compassionate decisions that you can. You can't *not* do that anyway, but the way is easier if we release resistance.

In truth, decisions happen, but they are not made.

We don't have to believe in a character for there to be an ongoing *experience* of a character. It's a joke to say it, but "There's no center in the center!" What we refer to as "a character" is just a loose arrangement of symbiotic conditioning. The experience of a character is inevitable, even though it is simultaneously spontaneous and transitory.

524. A make-believe character can never "surrender to" relativity any more than it can gain weight or grow taller. It's an *illusion!*

525. This teaching is not a character's tool to *bypass* relativity. This teaching empowers us to *embrace* relativity—regardless of its apparent content.

526. As seekers, our foremost desire is to *get rid of* an enemy that doesn't exist to begin with.

527. In the end, the "witness" is seen to be just another thought.

528. Unconscious Awakeness is the "state" of our misidentifying Divinity as a character. *Conscious* Awakeness is what remains upon Divinity's "waking up" to that very illusion.

529. The personification of divinity is fine as long as it's helpful. Prayer is simply an acknowledgement of the paradox of part-ness and wholeness. But if we use the idea to strengthen the sense of separation, then we are back in the middle of the Bubble of Self-Reflection.

530. So far as I can see, the "purpose" of life is to enjoy the sense of being.

531. Awakening is typically an event, although the

event probably will not include angels and trumpets and fireworks. Even if it does, we may not remember them because the character is never in attendance at awakenings.

Conversely, I consider enlightenment to be something that occurs gradually as the character-that-never-was is nonetheless *unbuilt*.

532. First, we pretend that there are impediments to living freely, and then we strive to overcome them. It all makes for a good story, but it generates an awful lot of suffering.

533. We are accustomed to praying for a change in our conditions. Perhaps we should instead pray for a change in our conditioning.

534. Hope is always a story of future. It's comparing

What Is with what isn't, and What Is always comes up short. In Reality, there is no such thing as future or comparison. There is only This-As-It-Is-Right-Now. Hope is a time-based argument with Now, which indicates that it's delusional.

535. However, apparent human beings generally vote for comfort over truth. The sad irony is that only the hard truth brings ultimate comfort.

536. The world rises to meet our view. When I change where I am looking *from*, what I am looking *at* changes.

If I view the world from a character's point of view, I find a world of confusion, suffering, and desperation. When I view the world *as* Wholeness *from* Wholeness, I find heaven on earth.

Naturally the unit cannot recognize heaven, because the unit is the very thing standing in the way of it.

537. In the absence of comparison, there is no suffering.

538. Given that What Is *already is,* it seems a bit late in the game to argue with it.

539. "Unit overwhelm" is the term I use to describe the loss of clarity that occurs when the character's concerns and fears stand at the forefront of our attention. It comes from attachment to our ideas of how things should be.

540. Whatever you put your attention on will expand in your experience. I'm not talking about so-called "manifestation"; I'm talking about whether we see a glass of water as being half full or half empty. Our responses to various situations unfold to meet what we *think* is going on, not what really *is* going on.

541. We tend to get wrapped up in the *content* of experience. Try inquiring into what it is that is *experiencing* the content instead.

542. One of the foundations of fear is the belief that you know what is good for "you," by which I mean that *unit*. You don't.

543. Notice that when one worry lifts, the dream just plugs another one in its place. These units are inherently unsatisfiable. Recognizing this dead-end is the beginning of moving beyond all dead ends.

544. We are not going to graduate from all identification and concern with the unit. If we did, the unit would very shortly die.

545. The only true thing is You. All that appears to happen is just a flicker of light over the stillness of a great lake.

546. Suffering is an alarm bell announcing that you are dreaming. Pain is pain and must be borne. But why suffer from *what isn't?*

547. We don't suffer from the thoughts we *have*; we suffer from the thoughts we *believe*. In that same way, we don't suffer from our conditions; we suffer from our beliefs *about* our conditions.

548. Buddha had his Four Noble Truths. I'm not in that league, so here are my four *ig*noble truths:

We make stuff up.

We *believe* what we just made up.

We *suffer* because we believe the stuff we just made up.

We come to spirituality to try to *overcome* the suffering we experience because we believe what we just made up.

549. Seekers are *addicts*. Our core addiction is to thought, which gives rise to a sense of separation. We are addicted to that *sense* of separation. We are *slaves* to the *sense* of individuality. We roll up our sleeves, take the needle, and violently *use* "our" self-image, beliefs, and opinions, to "prove" not only that we *are* but that in fact we are *special* and that our thoughts represent truth.

We pick up "our" views and positions right off the street and then aggressively use them to "prove" that we are *right* and to "illustrate" what pitiful victims we are. Are you not *tired* of this circular nonsense, Awakeness?

550. The desire for a *different* What Is to replace *this* What-Is-As-It-Is-Right-Now is the architect of all your suffering.

551. Perhaps the most challenging part of overcoming suffering is finding the willingness to give it up. Life has been a wild ride, but we've grown rather *fond* of that wildness. It may be awful, but the awfulness is *exciting*! There can be reckless joy in it or exquisite pain. We may start to feel that perhaps peace is not all that it's cracked up to be.

Peace can be unnervingly *steady* for a character, especially one used to being a cowboy. What harm could there be in believing *one little thought*? No one will even know! Unconsciousness beckons, and more often than not, we follow.

Hear this, and hear it well: many awaken, but precious few *clear*.

552. When the dream comes to an end, who is there to be hurt? In a perfect world, what is it that needs to be fixed? Is Oneness in danger from the Awakeness from which it arose?

553. If you want to know the truth, close your eyes and carefully examine the content of your mind; note what it is you *think* should be happening. Then open your eyes and notice what is *actually* happening. If the two versions are not in perfect alignment, then your viewpoint is that of your imaginary character.

554. Resistance is a defense mechanism that helps establish and protect the *sense* of individuality. As long as there is resistance to what is happening, there is identification with a character. In the absence of believing thought, there is no character and no problem.

555. If it is severe enough, the suffering that arises from the sense of separation will ultimately drive us to an asylum, self-harm, or spirituality. Though we may have the ears that will at some point be able to hear the truth, we might not yet be open enough to accept it. Be willing to *endure* the suffering that cannot yet be *embraced.* Transformation is never instantaneous.

556. Allow suffering to be your friend; it will push you back into the clarity you seek.

557. You already *are* Awakeness. Can you, Awakeness, *not* be "awake?" *Stand as Awakeness right now* and tell me about your problems. Can you find any?

No character, no problem. No problem, no character.

558. Intense experience spurs identification with a make-believe character. This misidentification automatically spawns the false experiencing of time, hence a dream of past and future, which is where all troubles live.

559. A unit is not living life. The unit is *being* lived *by* Life.
There are no rules.

560. Acceptance, as it's generally conceived, is a relative coping mechanism that enables an imaginary character to "allow" the Inevitable.

When you realize that you are unconditional acceptance itself, there's no need for you to accept anything because it's seen that everything has *already* been accepted. If it is "here," then it has already been pre-approved—*by You.*

561. The term "spiritual oscillation" refers to the pendulum of attention moving back and forth between believing in thought and seeing through it.

Having seen through false beliefs, all that's left is the silent verbness of the "Great Okayness," which is also known as the "Great Unknowing." It's a low-grade level of bliss, but nothing like the hyper-bliss state seekers imagine. It's also steady, whereas hyper-bliss comes and goes regularly.

562. Cultivate the willingness to be content with things as they are. If Awakeness had a vocabulary, disappointment would not be in it. This moment, exactly as it is, must be the *uncontested* moment.

563. Awakening is not about the character and its automated whims. It's about Awakeness becoming willing to let go of *projection* in favor of *experiencing*.

564. When Fredness was looking for a way out of suffering and faced with the options of extinction vs. suffering, it appears that the imaginary character "chose" extinction.

But who or what was it that "surrendered" to circumstances? It is the Absolute that surrenders to the relative instead.

565. If we are ever to be free, we will have to see through the delusion that the world must meet our conditions for us to be happy.

566. You can't treat relativity symptomatically. You can only address relativity by seeing that there is no sufferer. This doesn't mean that there is no suffering; it just means that it's not mine.

Characters demand to be the *experiencers* of the Great Okayness rather than the *Knowers* of the Great

Okayness. Be willing to see that such demands cannot be met. The unit is inherently unsatisfiable, so regardless of any boon, it will not be happy or feel complete.

567. The Great Okayness is not about peaks and troughs of suffering. It is contentedness with the continuous moving and morphing of What Is, a self-effulgent Knowing that all is well.

568. We don't choose to become seekers, and we don't choose our path. Seeking *happens*, and our path chooses *us*.

569. Does it feel like you're losing control? You can't lose what you never had. We don't "give up control" as we awaken. What we're giving up is merely the illusory *sense* of control.

We don't have to "let go" of the reins, but we must let go of the idea that we *ever held* the reins to begin with.

570. The paradox of intention is that the less I pretend to direct, the less I pretend to suffer.

571. Identification as a character who wants more, who fears loss or change, guarantees suffering. Accepting relativity on its own terms frees you from comparing What Is with *what isn't.*

572. We can make all of the choices that we want, but we can't choose what we choose.

573. Freedom from the "unsatisfiable me" begins with

the recognition that this body-mind unit can never be satisfied anyway, so why try? Why not let what happens *happen*?

It's a dream character that believes it has free will and self-control. Choice happens—only you aren't the one who makes it.

574. There is nothing that a pretend-character can do to directly affect or alter relativity-ness. However, there seems to be some utterly paradoxical form of *influencing* the dream. It makes no sense at all. I don't understand it; I'm just reporting it.

This *apparent* influence is determined by where we're looking *from*—whether from the depth of Awakeness or from the eyes of the me-character. A character always has a point of view. Awakeness has no viewpoint.

575. Recognize that *this* Way is the *only* Way. Just recognizing the truth of this single fact—*even intellectually*—is, by itself, infinitely freeing.

576. There are three types of witnessing. First, there is witnessing-with-involvement. Next, there is witnessing-without-involvement. Finally, it is noticed that there *is* *no* witness.

The highest state is devoid of experience, experiencing, or an experiencer. The lack of an experience is not in itself an experience. The highest state is not a state. It is Void.

577. We can either look at the world *as* a unit, or we can look at the world *through* a unit. If we identify *as* a unit, we're going to encounter endless beliefs, opinions, positions—and suffering.

If we recognize that we are That which *uses* the unit to experience ourSelf objectively, then we are free. The unit is used as either a telescope or a microscope. We zoom in, or we zoom out, dependent upon the direction of the Happening.

578. Real freedom comes from the abandonment of any attempt to *understand* This.

579. Freedom from imagination is when we live *as What Is* instead of *in* what isn't.

580. We are neither *on* nor *of* this planet. So how deeply are we going to allow any arising on this planet to affect us? We're going to allow it to affect us precisely to the same degree that we believe we are a *thing* on or of this world.

581. Freedom from imagination means that we "get this." We can't *not* have this experience because...here it is. But we don't have to *sweat* this experience because in the truest sense it is not real. It *looks* like a duck; it *walks* and *talks* like a duck; but it is *not* a duck!

582. We may not be able to prevent the character's natural resistance to a given event or circumstance, but we *can* stop running away from events and circumstances.

583. Whenever we are focused on the content of this arising, we are lending it credence. When we pull our focus *away* from the content of this arising, we are drawing attention away from illusion and placing it onto truth. Recognizing the mechanisms of the dream is vital to our becoming free of them.

584. In the absence of thought, what's wrong with This?

Let's reconsider our allegiance to thought and simply relax for a while. We can always reclaim stress and worry if we miss them too much.

585. The dream of self-agency is entirely false. The Happening is nothing more than conditioning rising to meet conditions over and over again, everywhere we look. There are *no doers*, just apparent *doing*.

It's all just an *apparent happening*. Allow *This* to be *As It Is*. We have no choice in the matter anyway. IT does what IT does.

586. A good question to ask yourself is, "Am I consciously awake to this present arising?"

587. I like to think of this teaching as being the study and practice of "*Duh!*"

588. This practice is simply about noticing What Is. When we see What Is clearly enough, we notice there is no such thing as "What Isn't." Look for yourself, and see that there is neither comparison nor alternative to What Is. *This* This is IT.

589. We pin all of our hopes on some desire or goal, but once attained, we see that "it" is still not the "it" we so desperately want.

The mechanism of the dream is to continually pull us out of the Here and Now and into a future vision that's an improvement over This. The story of future satisfaction is futile and endless.

590. You are not *experiencing* the present moment. You *are* the present moment. You are not limited to This, but This is not other than you.

591. We are not awake; we are Awake*ness*. Awakeness is a verb; thus enlightenment is about right now*ing— only*. We are only awake (or not) to *this* arising right here, right now.

592. We must come to terms with Life As It Is. The past is *so* over!

593. The hope or expectation of an awakening experience or greater clarity later only results in moving backward because both are a story of future. The so-called "future" never comes. Are you looking to awaken or gain clarity *somewhere else in the future*?

STOP!

It's *now* or never, *here* or nowhere.

594. Most of us are very lazy spiritual seekers. We have a sense of entitlement when it comes to nonduality—as if we are *owed* the easy knowledge for which countless people have suffered and died. This world owes you *nothing*, nothing at all. We live in and as the lush bounty of Maya and simultaneously whine about it.

595. We always already have all the information that we need to awaken—in fact, way *more* than enough. Insight comes on an as-needed basis. If you want to Know yourself *as* This, put your *attention* on This.

596. The experience of an imaginary, independent character will always take place within the boundaries of a story. You are beyond both limits and levels.

597. Memory is a projection of an idea that doesn't exist, any more than an idea of future exists. No effort is needed to live in the Now because there is nothing other than Now. Relax into this.

598. When you initially come to see True Nature, you may notice some changes in the unit's behavior. Or not. The personal conditioning (thoughts, opinions, and behavior patterns) that are "supposed" to fall away will do so, but it is likely to be rather minimal in the beginning. There will *always* be at least some conditioning (probably a *lot*) which is not seen through.

Don't allow best to become the enemy of better. Wherever you are *right now* is exactly where you *must* be until you aren't. If there is improvement, fine. If there isn't, fine.

599. Awakening is not about whether or not we were clear or cloudy in the past or might be in the future.

Neither past nor future exist for you, only for the character within the story of relativity-ness.

600. Awakening is an *ongoing revelation* that can only occur through *ongoing humility.* There is enormous arrogance within the seeking community. I know that because there are regular sightings of it here. So what? These units do what they do. *Notice* what they do and move on. There is no need to judge them and no point either.

601. If you're not happy with what you have, you're not going to be happy with what you get. Persistent unhappiness is a symptom of misunderstanding. It doesn't get any better than *This* because there is *only* This, by which I mean *this* This.

602. Here are some lines of inquiry you could investigate to your advantage.

Who is it that is dissatisfied with this moment? Is the present moment really unsatisfactory? *Who is it* that knows that the answer is no? Is there really a "me" here? Is it possible for "me" to know the truth?

603. As long as there is craving for the character to understand *This*, you are within the Bubble of Self-Reflection. Freedom comes only with the willingness to forgo understanding and call off the search. Otherwise, the itch to seek will return.

604. Let us not be concerned about the thoughts we think. I mean, *who cares?* Let us concern ourSelves here with the thoughts we believe. "Therein lies the rub," wrote Shakespeare. His *wakefulness* was regularly showing Itself.

605. There is no cure for what is already going on. But this moment's patterns are not necessarily a predictor of the next moment's patterns. Just sit without expectations. *Be* the Now that You *are*.

606. What I call "Attention Practice" is simply noticing ourSelf. We simply notice that there is presently a sense of existence. I call it the sense of being. It's the same sense that was there when we were children. It never leaves, and it never changes. Simply noticing that present sense of existence makes us stop and pay attention to Attention.

Paying attention to Attention doesn't help us see clearly "later," whatever "later" might be. The act of Attention paying attention to Attention *is* Realization itself.

607. *Who is it* that wants to have a deeper experience of oneness, of awakening? You're trying to get an imaginary character to reach a deeper level of a concept *you* have conjured up!

608. What you're looking *with* is what you're looking *for*.

609. This is all process without goals. We are already *here*, and there is no there *there*. The only thing we need to accept is that there is Only This As It Is, whether we accept it or not.

610. Fear arises from thought, not experience. As Sailor Bob says, "What's wrong with right now unless you think about it?"

611. This moment cannot be any other than the way it is. It is the flowering of the Inevitable. Our job is simply to Know this. See that You are the *present* Presence.

612. An honest eye sees No-thing even as it sees everything.

613. The wellspring of awakening is deep, inexplicable gratitude for What Is.

614. The desire for intimacy is the call for Conscious Awakeness to know itself objectively and experience itself as "other," which is fine. In truth, there is nothing *but* intimacy. THIS *This* is always the Self experiencing the Self.

615. Happiness is a moment lived without expectation.

616. What changes after awakening is not what you're looking *at* but where you're looking *from*. Looking from Awakeness, you find the perfection that is Isness.

617. If you are not in a state of gratitude, you are in a state of misidentification.

618. The gratitude we feel upon awakening is gratitude that can no longer be withheld.

619. I've become a much better person than I ever intended to be.

620. *Oneness* does not mean *sameness*. I love mySelf equally in union and diversity.

621. After awakening, we often feel the pull to help so-called "others," whether we want to or not. We can't help but become Conscious Bodhisattvas. Let us determine not to be stupid about it. And most of all, let us examine closely whether we are trying to *help* or *show off.*

622. *What* is reading this sentence? *Check*!

623. The apex of human experience is Awakeness *consciously* living through a unit. It is the simultaneous experience of limitation and infinity.

624. We have all won the lottery. We are all Awakeness. We all abide in a state of pristine perfection. It doesn't get any better than this! But few will recognize this truth, and far fewer still will come to embody IT.

There is only Love, and You are That.

- No Ending -

Printed in Great Britain
by Amazon

78688227R00142